Mother Nature's Shopping List

ALSO BY MICHAEL D. SHOOK

Legal Briefs

By Any Other Name

It's About Time (with Robert L. Shook)

The Book of Odds (with Robert L. Shook)

Mother Nature's Shopping List

A Buying Guide for
Environmentally
Concerned Consumers

MICHAEL D. SHOOK

A CITADEL PRESS BOOK
PUBLISHED BY CAROL PUBLISHING GROUP

A Citadel Press Book
Published by Carol Publishing Group
Citadel Press is a registered trademark of Carol Communications, Inc.
Editorial Offices: 600 Madison Avenue, New York, N.Y. 10022
Sales and Distribution Offices: 120 Enterprise Avenue, Secaucus, N.J. 07094
In Canada: Canadian Manda Group, One Atlantic Avenue, Suite 105, Toronto, Ontario M6K 3E7
Queries regarding rights and permissions should be addressed to Carol Publishing Group, 600 Madison Avenue, N.Y. 10022

♲ This book is printed on recycled paper.

Carol Publishing Group books are available at special discounts for bulk purchases, sales promotion, fund-raising, or educational purposes. Special editions can be created to specifications. For details, contact: Special Sales Department, Carol Publishing Group, 120 Enterprise Avenue, Secaucus, N.J. 07094

Book design by Jessica Shatan

Manufactured in the United States of America
10 9 8 7 6 5 4 3 2 1

Library of Congress Cataloging-in-Publication Data

Shook, Michael D.
    Mother Nature's shopping list : a buying guide for environmentally concerned consumers / by Michael D. Shook.
        p.   cm
    "A Citadel Press book."
    ISBN 0-8065-1633-X
    1. Environmental protection—Citizen participation.   2. Green products.   I. Title.
    TD171.7.S53   1995
    363.7'0525—dc20   94-45491
                                                                        CIP

This book is dedicated to Mother Nature—
it couldn't have been done without her.

Contents

Acknowledgments

I am grateful to the following people who helped me in some way with the researching and preparation of this book: Crested Butte Forest Rescue; High Country Citizens Alliance; Sarah Hamilton; Ido Ziv; Chuck Cerasoli; my agent, Jeff Herman; and most important, my father, Robert Shook.

And special thanks to Maggie Abel and my editor, Bruce Shostak, both of whom are exceptional in their areas of expertise.

Introduction

Mother Nature herself would urge you to take this list with you on any big shopping spree. In fact, she'd probably insist that you abide by it even on a casual errand to the corner drugstore or convenience mart.

I urge you to follow the recommendations in this book when you buy practically everything—whether it's something big, like a house or a new car, or something small, such as a bottle of shampoo or a package of napkins.

Much of what I tell you in this book ends up being good for your pocketbook as well as the environment. Hundreds of tips here serve both purposes. In other cases, I advise you to do what's good for the environment—even when there won't be a savings in terms of dollars. But you'll be doing the *right thing*—and this is what matters most! My focus is on the long term, doing what must be done to protect our environment rather than looking for the easiest or cheapest solution or purchase without regard for the consequences.

Every one of us must pitch in and do his or her share, because, sadly, a lot of bad things are being done to destroy our beautiful Earth. And like it or not, we can't afford to ruin what we've got, because for the time being—and, most likely, forever—this is the only inhabitable planet we've got. Please, do what you can do to keep it beautiful and inhabitable.

Throughout this book I will remind you to adhere religiously to the *Three R's,* which are *Reduce, Reuse,* and *Recycle.* Obedience to these crucial rules is essential for every person in the world. Here's a brief explanation of the Three R's in the order of their importance:

Reduce

The most important step in diminishing your negative impact on the environment is thinking before you buy. For instance, by shunning products that pollute or create waste, you lessen your ecological impact. At the same time, you voice a powerful statement manufacturers are sure to hear. You speak even louder when you let a manufacturer know your motives for avoiding its products (e.g., animal testing, wasteful use of a nonrenewable resource, too much packaging, etc.) And by spreading the word to your friends and neighbors, your efforts multiply.

You can think of this step as "*pre*cycling," avoiding wasteful products from the start, rather than having to go through the next steps of reusing or recycling, or, worse, discarding.

Reuse

This is the consumer's second most important step. Rather than using a product only once before recycling or discarding, reuse it as many times as possible. Keep this in mind when shopping by selecting products that can be reused. For instance, to store food in the refrigerator, purchase a reclosable plastic container instead of plastic or aluminum foil. Doing so saves money in the long run, and most important, it saves landfill space.

Another part of reusing is buying products packaged in

recycled materials. This saves precious resources while stimulating the demand for recycled goods.

Recycle

After avoiding wasteful products and reusing as much as possible, the third alternative is recycling. It's plain to see that discarding recyclable items throws away scarce natural resources. Recycling also creates six times as many jobs as do landfills or incineration plants.

Although these Three R's are not the ones you learned in elementary school, they are just as important, especially as you join the crusade to save our environment. I ask you to spread the word to family members, friends, co-workers—everybody. We are running out of time, and unless everybody pitches in, we will all suffer.

Although saving the environment is of worldwide concern, as Americans, we must lead the crusade. Why? Because, our affluence causes us to consume so much more than our share of the earth's resources. Consequently, we have an obligation to do more than our share to preserve those resources. As a leader among nations, the United States has the opportunity to serve as a shining example. The world's destiny rests upon how we perform our responsibility.

Mother Nature's Shopping List

1 The Supermarket

Since most of the products we buy are purchased at the supermarket, this is perhaps the place where intelligent shopping can make the biggest difference. The following is what you should look for aisle by aisle while shopping for groceries, as well as what products you should avoid.

Produce

Despite everything you think you know about the nutritional value of fruits and vegetables, most of the produce bought at the grocery store has a tremendous impact on the environment—and possibly on your health. The 1.5 billion pounds of pesticides our farmers use to kill bugs, fungi, and weeds each year has made the Environmental Protection Agency declare pesticide use one of our country's worst environmental and health problems. The pesticides pollute our soil and groundwater as well as end up in the food on our table.

Buy Locally Grown Produce

Locally grown produce isn't shipped long distances, so it gets to you without using extra fossil fuel and creating more air pollution (the way produce shipped long distances will do). Since locally grown fruits and vegetables don't have to wait as long before being eaten they don't need all the pesticides used to preserve produce transported long distances. And because they are fresher, they retain more of their nutrients.

In many parts of the United States, fruits and vegetables are not grown during the winter months and must be shipped in. This doesn't mean you can't have your own homegrown fruits and veggies. By preserving your fruits and vegetables at home through canning or drying, you can enjoy locally grown fruits and vegetables throughout the year.

Pesticides are nothing more than toxic chemicals used on our fruits and vegetables to prolong storage life and to keep produce blemish free. Although only a tiny fraction of the pesticides used have been tested by the FDA, most are widely believed to contain harmful carcinogens.

Processed Fruits and Vegetables

If you have the choice, avoid canned or frozen fruits and vegetables that have been processed. They are overpackaged and often contain additives such as sodium, sugar, and artificial colors and flavors which worsen their nutritional value.

Buy Fresh, Organically Grown Produce

Produce that is grown organically is grown without the use of chemical fertilizers or pesticides. It can cost a little more but is worth the extra money because it is usually fresh and carries no chemical residues. It is available at farmers' markets, co-ops, and many large grocery stores.

Milk and Eggs

Unless your area recycles HDPE (high density polyethylene, i.e. milk jugs) plastic, always buy milk in waxed cardboard boxes because the cardboard has less impact on the environment. (PET—polyethylene terephthalate—is the plastic that soft drink and bottled water containers are made of.)

Commercial milk also contains a genetically engineered drug derived from protein called Bovine Growth Hormone.

Bovine Growth Hormone has been known to cause Mastitis, an inflammation of the mammary gland, in humans (mostly female). It can also give cows udder infections, which are treated with antibiotics, which in turn leads to increased levels of antibiotic residue in the milk we drink.

There are alternatives to dairy milk. Many companies now make milk from soy and rice products that are available at many grocery and health food stores.

Purchase eggs in recyclable and/or biodegradable cardboard containers or recycled materials; stay away from foam. And if at all possible, buy organic eggs; the chickens are treated humanely and their feed is organically grown without chemical additives. The birds also receive no antibiotics or drugs.

Cereals

Just about all dry breakfast cereals are packaged the same way, in a recycled paperboard box with a sealed plastic bag. Some, however, are packaged with virgin fibers. These, of course, are the ones to avoid. Look on the box to see if the manufacturer has indicated that the packaging is made from recycled materials.

Buy the largest box whenever possible (your unit cost will also be lower). Be sure to stay away from the little individually wrapped boxes of cereal—that's a lot of packaging for a small portion of cereal. If your local supermarket sells cereal in the bulk section or just by the bag, take advantage. You will avoid cardboard packaging and save money in the process. The same principles apply when buying hot cereals.

Beverages

If you're like most Americans you buy a lot in the beverage department at the supermarket. The average American drinks about 47 gallons of soda a year, compared to 37 gallons of plain tap water. Along with the containers for dozens of other beverages on the market, this amounts to a lot of solid waste. The following are some facts you should know about choosing specific types of beverages.

Bottled Water

The bottled water phenomenon of yesteryear's elite class has grown to include millions of Americans. Although most people don't think of this beverage as having a huge environmental impact, it does.

Unlike your tap water, bottled water doesn't usually come from a nearby source. The energy and pollution costs in shipping and packaging are extensive, and most of the water is packaged in nonbiodegradable plastic and glass bottles that further contribute to our solid waste problem.

Before converting over to bottled water check your local water authority to see if your tap water is safe. If you insist on buying bottled water, buy it from the closest source available to avoid excess transportation costs and make sure the bottle is recyclable in your area. The most environmentally sound method of buying bottled water is to use a home-delivery service that will bring refillable containers to your home and carry away the empties on a weekly schedule.

> ❧ The Green Rule of Thumb When Buying Beverages
>
> • Only buy beverages in 100 percent recyclable containers that you are certain can be recycled in your area.
>
> • Don't buy products that have extra layers of unnecessary packaging. This includes those plastic "yokes" that hold six packs together and plastic layers of shrink wrapping.
>
> • Buy in bulk whenever possible. If you need small containers to travel with or take to lunch, buy a set of reusable plastic bottles instead of juice boxes or other small containers.
>
> • When buying powdered beverages, buy them in large containers instead of individual packets.
>
> • If your area recycles PET plastic (used in soda bottles) or HDPE (used in milk and water jugs) only buy clear containers unless you're sure they will recycle colored plastic bottles. If they don't recycle plastic, stick with aluminum or glass containers.
>
> • Always choose beverages packaged by local bottlers if possible. They require less pollution and energy to get to the shelves than bottles from faraway sources.

We drink about two billion gallons of bottled water a year. If your tap water is safe to drink (most is), by all means drink it. Bottled water costs around $1.15 per gallon. Compare that to tap water, which costs on the average $1.28 per thousand gallons. This makes tap water about 900 times cheaper!

Juice Boxes
Unfortunately, those tiny rectangular boxes with the built-in straws have swept across the country at an alarming rate.

Because they are lightweight, convenient, and nearly indestructible, they are very popular. They are made of three layers of packaging: paperboard, polyethylene plastic, and aluminum foil. These three materials in a single package make them virtually nonrecyclable.

The best alternative is to buy a set of small plastic reusable containers in which to transport your juice instead of these aseptic packages that only take up landfill space. This will allow you to buy juice in bulk and therefore save you money and all of us precious landfill space.

Another substitute for juice boxes is to buy juice in smaller readily recyclable containers such as steel, aluminum, or glass that many manufacturers are starting to use. This, however, isn't exactly the greenest thing you can do; they still require a lot of energy and pollution to manufacture.

Pasta, Beans, and Grains

These foods represent some of the most environmentally sound foods available at the grocery store, and, because they are good sources of protein, I include them just before the meat department. They are low on the food chain and very healthy, containing, in addition to protein, complex carbohydrates, fiber, vitamins, and minerals.

Although these foods are good for many reasons, the ways they get into your hands can also be harsh to the environment. Some companies overpackage them in extra layers of paper and plastic, and many farming techniques implement dangerous pesticides to make the end product look better.

When choosing pasta, grains, and beans, look for ones with simple and natural ingredients that required minimal processing. If possible, look for products that are organically grown and are sold in the least amount of packaging. Many grocery stores as well as health-food stores have a bulk section that will save you trash and cash.

Meats

A growing number of Americans are eating less meat or eliminating it from their diets altogether and becoming vegetarians. Today there are more than 7.5 million vegetarians in America. And people aren't just eating less meat for health reasons—they are doing so with environmental objectives in mind. The following is a gloomy list of statistics on the wasteful meat industry.

- If Americans reduced their red meat intake by only 10 percent, the savings of grains and soybeans could feed all the people who starve to death each year in the world: an estimated 60 million lives. After all, nearly 40 percent of the world's grain is fed to livestock. (Source: John Robbins, *Diet for a New America,* Stillpoint, 1987.)

- Each year the average American eats 178 pounds of red meat and poultry. (Source: *Worldwatch* magazine.)

- An estimated 20 vegetarians can be fed on the land required to feed one person who eats meat. It also takes 16 pounds of grain and soybeans, 2,500 gallons of water, and the energy equivalent of 1 gallon of gasoline to produce just 1 pound of beef. (Source: *50 Simple Things You Can Do to Save the Earth,* The EarthWorks Group. Earthworks Press, Berkley, CA, 1989.)

- It takes 6.9 pounds of grain to produce one pound of pork in the United States. Pork is also a tremendous

waste of energy. It takes 15 times the energy to supply one pound of pork to U.S. consumers as compared to the energy it takes for every pound of rice, potatoes, fruits, or vegetables.
(Source: *Worldwatch* Magazine.)

• Since 1960, more than 25 percent of the forests of Central America have been cleared to create pasture land for grazing cattle.
(Source: Jeremy Rifkin, *Beyond Beef.* Dutton, New York, NY, 1992.)

• The typical four-ounce hamburger patty represents about 55 square feet of tropical forest. This typical small area of rain forest contains one 60-foot-tall tree; 50 saplings and seedlings representing 20 to 30 different tree species; two pounds of insects representing thousands of creatures and more than a hundred different species; a pound of mosses, fungi, and microorganisms; and a section of the feeding zone of dozens of birds, reptiles, and mammals, some of them very rare.
(Source: Rainforest Action Network.)

For those of you who continue to eat meat, choose free-range products. The animals aren't kept in tight quarters and bypass steroid injections. They are also not fed pesticide-laden food.

To avoid excess packaging, buy the largest quantities available. Also, make sure the meat you buy is from the United States. If it is not, chances are part of a rain forest was cut down to create pasture land for grazing.

Condiments and Preserves

As with most other goods in the supermarket, the important thing to look for when choosing between condiments

is the packaging. Unfortunately, most companies have come
out with jellies and ketchups in plastic squeezable bottles—
an environmental nightmare. Most are contrived with several layers of plastic, making them just about impossible to
recycle. A few claim to be recyclable but are in fact impossible to recycle in most areas. They are not biodegradable
(your great-great-grandchildren will have them around), and
they are very polluting to manufacture.

Traditional glass jars and bottles are the way to go. They
are easy to recycle and less polluting to manufacture. If you
must rely on squeezable plastic bottles (some people aren't
coordinated enough to pour), then by all means don't throw
them away. Instead, buy the biggest glass container available
and refill your plastic squeezable.

✖ Minimize Your Food Waste

• Look for ways to avoid throwing out food. For instance,
sour milk can be used for sour-milk pancakes; aging bananas
are great for banana bread.

• If you buy more food than you know you are going to use
immediately, freeze some for later use.

• Keep track of what's in your refrigerator, and eat perishable
foods as soon as possible.

• Only serve yourself what you can eat. It is much harder
and less appetizing to save leftovers after they have been sitting on a half-eaten plate.

• Establish a compost pile so your uneaten food will not go
to waste (see Chapter 9).

• Arrange to donate leftover food from a big event to a
homeless shelter.

Pet Supplies

Dog and Cat Foods

The most important thing to look for when buying commercial dog and cat foods is, of course, the packaging. Avoid pet foods packaged in single servings. Choose dry foods available in bulk. Big recyclable paper bags are great, but avoid foil wrappers or paper wrappings that are lined with foil.

Unfortunately, pets are subject to the same environmental hazards in their diets that people face. Although the quality may vary, many foods that go into pet menus come from the same sources that humans use. And so the same environmental dangers are present: excessive energy is used in the manufacture, plants are often grown in nutrient-weak soil, water used in the processing may be contaminated by runoff chemicals, and drugs administered to animal food sources may be passed on to your pet. Search carefully for the right brand for your pet. Speciality or premium brands rather than standard supermarket brands may be the best answer. Many are careful about the ingredients they use, and have designed specific products to meet nutritional needs at various stages in your pet's life. Although they are more expensive per pound, they are more nutritionally concentrated and efficiently digested, so your dog or cat will not require as much to eat, and hence save resources, energy, and time spent with the pooper scooper. If your local supermarket does not carry these foods, contact your veterinarian or pet shop.

If you would like your dog or cat to eat a vegetarian diet, your local health food store may have some regional brands or more information. But be careful. Most veterinarians agree that cats and dogs need meat products for a well balanced diet.

Flea and Tick Control

Commercial products to control fleas and ticks on your pet are highly toxic to the environment. Their manufacture releases harsh chemicals into our air and water. The safest way to control fleas and ticks is to abstain from commercial products that are highly toxic and instead use natural remedies.

Prevention is the best way to reduce your pet's vulnerability to fleas and ticks. Keep your pet in top health, since parasites are less attracted to healthy animals, and minimize the risk of exposure to fleas and ticks. For instance, during tick season keep your pet out of long grass and out of brushy, wooded areas where ticks are abundant. Bathing your pet frequently with any shampoo will help kill fleas and any mild infestations. Also, groom your pet frequently to keep its oils distributed and skin healthy. Another great preventive measure is to add brewer's yeast to your pet's food. It helps deter fleas and contains vitamins and protein.

If your pet does happen to get fleas or ticks (most do at some point in their lives), there are a few things you can do yourself to combat the problem. Flea combs work by trapping fleas as you comb the animal. To kill the fleas you've caught, dip the comb in a dish of soapy water. Flea combs are available at most shops and some supermarkets.

A less harmful, nontraditional remedy repels pests by simply making your pet less attractive to them as a breeding or feasting ground. Collect the clean rinds of your breakfast citrus fruit, and boil them over low heat in a small amount of water. After the resulting substance cools, use it to give your pet a most unusual massage, then rinse. Fleas will flee and ticks will take off when they encounter your dog or cat's citrus-oil-coated fur.

Flea Combs

—Breeders Equipment Co., (215) 233-0799
—Petco Animal Supplies, (800) 765-9878

If you feel the need to buy a commercial product, look for ones that are nontoxic with the least amount of packaging. Also look for brands that don't test their ingredients on animals, usually in an inhumane way, killing them afterwards. The safest commercial products for your dog and the environment are nontoxic, cruelty-free herbal formulas. The repellents are made from the oil of plants such as cedarwood, eucalyptus, citronella, and bay leaves. Some shampoos use soaps to kill existing fleas and ticks and herbs to repel newcomers.

Nontoxic, Cruelty-Free, Herbal Flea and Tick Formulas

—Green Ban (herbal powder and shampoo), (319) 227-7996
—Natural Animal (herbal collars, spray and shampoo), order from Baubiologie Hardware, (408) 372-6826
—Natural Animal (herbal food supplements), order from Gardens Alive!, (812) 623-3800
—No Common Scents (herbal flea oil), (513) 767-4261
—PetGuard (herbal collars, powder, shampoo), (800) 423-7544
—Safer (spray, shampoo), (800) 423-7544

If you use it carefully, insects can be killed using Pyrethrum, an insect powder made from chrysanthemums. However, it can be poisonous if ingested.

PYRETHRUM AND OTHER NATURAL PRODUCTS

—ALL THE BEST PET CARE carries natural flea control remedies
and other products, (800) 962-8266.

—ECO-SAFE PRODUCTS, INC., makes natural pyrethrum-based flea
powder, (800) 274-7387.

—FRONTIER COOPERATIVE HERBS sells a variety of natural
products, (800) 669-3275.

—MORRILLS' NEW DIRECTIONS carries a wide variety of alternative
pet products. Call for a free copy of *Your Natural Pet Care
Catalogue,* (800) 368-5057.

—NATURAL ANIMAL pyrethrum powder, order from Gardens Alive!,
(812) 623-3800.

—PRISTINE PRODUCTS sells organic flea- and tick-control
products, combining food-grade diatomaceous earth and
natural pyrethrums, (602) 955-7031.

—RINGER CORP. makes Safer brand pest-control products, (800)
423-7544.

There is an alternative if all else fails. Two low-toxicity
chemicals called methoprene and phenoxycarb work mirac-
ulously well. These man-made substances do not extermi-
nate adult fleas but prohibit larvae from reaching maturity,
therefore ceasing reproduction.

INSECT GROWTH REGULATORS

—ZOECON manufactures Precor products, (800) 527-0512.

Getting rid of fleas can seem like an ongoing losing bat-
tle. If this is the case, it is probable that your house is in-

fested with fleas. They are most likely in your pet's bedding but love to reproduce in your carpet and furniture as well.

If this scenario seems all too familiar, pick up on your vacuuming! And don't forget the furniture and small inconspicuous crevices and cracks in your floor where they are likely hiding out. Also, be sure to empty your vacuum bag outside (unless of course you want them breeding underneath your sink as well). Confine your pet to only one sleeping quarter and wash and vacuum it religiously. Another great nonpoisonous method to kill fleas and larvae in infested areas is diatomaceous earth. It works by parching the fleas and their larvae, and it can be purchased in hardware, garden, pet, and some grocery stores.

Paper Products

Believe it or not, paper products pose a great threat to the environment and to your health. Despite the fact that paper degrades rather quickly, can be recycled, and comes from a natural resource, manufacturing it contaminates the environment enormously.

Turning trees into paper requires massive amounts of energy and pollution at every stage, especially during the process to break down wood pulp into wood fibers which releases many harsh chemicals. In 1989 alone, the paper industry in America released over 3.2 million lbs. of toxins into our environment. White paper is the result of a chlorine bleaching process containing highly toxic and carcinogenic dioxins that often end up in our water, food, and skin.

Chemicals are just part of the problem. Paper and pulp mills in this country cut down almost a billion trees a year. Most large paper companies clearcut (which indiscriminately slaughters trees regardless of age or size) a part of the forest, then attempt to restock the forest with selected species of trees. These young saplings are doused with toxic herbicides to prevent any other growth on the forest floor. This procedure greatly inhibits and harms the natural development of the entire ecosystem.

Paper also generates more solid waste than any other material in America. In 1995, it is estimated that almost 80 million tons of paper and paperboard contributed to our solid waste. That is about 38 percent of the total amount of waste generated!

The most important thing to remember when purchasing paper products is to look for products made from recycled paper and for products that are recyclable. Buy in bulk whenever possible to avoid excess packaging. To avoid dioxins, buy unbleached or chlorine-free paper products.

The following is a list of paper-product brands made from recycled paper and the companies that manufacture them. The products are made from a mixture of post-consumer waste (PCW) from curbside and community recycling programs and pre-consumer recovered industrial waste (PRE), which is excess paper generated during the manufacturing process.

—AWARE facial tissues, bath tissues, paper towels, and napkins (Ashdun Industries, (201) 944-2650).
—CAPRI, GAYETY, GENTLE TOUCH, NATURE'S CHOICE, AND PERT facial tissues, bath tissues, paper towels, and napkins (Pope & Talbot, Inc., (503) 228-9161).
—C.A.R.E. facial tissues, bath tissues, paper towels, coffee filters, and napkins (Ashdun Industries, (201) 944-2650).
—CASCADES facial tissues, bath tissues, paper towels, and napkins (Cascades Industries, (819) 363-2704).
—DOUCELLE bath tissues and kitchen towels (Cascades Industries, (819) 363-2704).   *(CONTINUED)*

—ENVIROCARE AND ENVIROQUEST facial tissues, bath tissues, paper towels, and napkins (Ashdun Industries (201) 944-2650).

—FOREVER GREEN, GREEN MEADOW, NEW DAY'S CHOICE, SAFE, AND TREE-FREE facial tissues, bath tissues, paper towels, and napkins (Statler Tissue Co., (617) 395-7770).

—GREEN FOREST bath tissues, napkins, and paper towels (Fort Howard Corp., (414) 435-8821).

—MOR-SOFT bath tissues and napkins, Rose Soft bath tissues, AND MORNING GLORY napkins (Morcon, Inc., (518) 677-8511).

—PROJECT GREEN facial tissues, bath tissues, paper towels, and napkins (Ashdun Industries, (201) 944-2650).

—START facial tissues, bath tissues, paper towels, and napkins (Orchids Paper Products Co., (714) 523-7881).

—TODAY'S CHOICE facial tissues, bath tissues, paper towels, and napkins (Confab Co., (714) 955-2690).

Avoid Styrofoam

Avoid using Styrofoam (polystyrene foam) for anything! Styrofoam is made from cancer-causing benzene. Benzene, which contains toxic chemicals containing carcinogens, is used to produce styrene, which is then blown up with HCFCs to create the foam. Furthermore, Styrofoam isn't biodegradable; the cup you used for coffee yesterday will still be sitting in a landfill when your great-grandchildren are around. If a disposable plate or cup is a must, ask for paper instead. Or better yet, bring your own coffee mug to work and to fast-food restaurants. This will reduce toxins in the atmosphere, save landfill space, and could, if more people did it, lower the prices at restaurants in the long run. Voice your protests to fast-food companies that use Styrofoam products—if enough customers do, they'll replace them with earth-friendly products. Remember McDonald's old Big Mac containers? You don't see them around anymore because McDonald's discontinued them and switched to paper.

Bring Your Own Bag

The average American consumes the equivalent of seven trees per year. There are simple solutions to reduce the number of trees cut. First of all, cut down on using paper products. For every 700 paper grocery bags *not* used, one 15- to 20-year-old tree will be left standing. Instead of using paper bags at the grocery store, bring a mesh one or a backpack. Or reuse the paper bags you took home yesterday for the next trip to the market. Some grocery stores even give you a five- to ten-cent reward for bringing your own bags.

Trash Bags

With the increasing volume of trash entering landfills each day, plastic trash bags pose a huge threat to the environment. They are polluting to manufacture and don't break down in landfills. Many companies have claimed their plastic bags are biodegradable, but for the most part those are false claims. Some of them do break down a little, but they still threaten our water sources. The manufacturing of plastic releases toxic chemicals into the air, coming back in the form of acid rain, which pollutes our water supply. The best alternative is to use recycled paper bags to take your trash out. You probably already have them from your last trip to the grocery anyway, so they're inexpensive (if not free) and they break down in landfills. If you can't tolerate small paper bags always buy recycled plastic bags. They are made with as much as 80 percent recycled plastic so they aren't as energy-intensive to manufacture and they don't use as much petroleum, a diminishing natural resource.

These companies make trash bags from recycled materials. Many of them make many different types of plastic bags: 33-gallon trash bags, tall kitchen bags, lawn-and-leaf bags, etc.

—AMWAY TRASH BAGS (Locate a local distributor in your phone book)
—FULL CIRCLE AND BEST BUY trash bags (Dyna-Pak Corp., (615) 762-4016)
—HARMONY AND RECYCLE 1 (North American Plastics Corp., (708) 896-6200)
—MR. NEAT BAGS AGAIN trash bags (Stout Plastics, (612) 881-8673)
—RENEW trash bags (Webster Industries, (508) 532-2000)

Plastic Containers

Although plastic is something to avoid for the most part, plastic food storage containers are an exception. Even though they don't degrade and are very polluting to manufacture, they save natural resources and landfill space in the long run.

Since they can be used over and over again, plastic food containers substitute for disposable plastic and aluminum foil used for wrapping foods. They will also save you money in the long run. A two-quart plastic container costs about the same as a disposable roll of plastic wrap (about $2.50), but will last for many years.

Cleaning Supplies

This aisle in the grocery story is perhaps the most environmentally hazardous of all. Most cleaning agents are highly toxic and contain harmful chemicals. For that reason many

❧ Tips to Conserve Energy in the Kitchen

• Believe it or not, microwave ovens use the same amount of energy as conventional ovens but cook most foods in half the time, thus using half the amount of energy.

• Quit peeking! Peeking in the oven when something is cooking wastes a tremendous amount of energy. Every time you open the door heat is lost and the food takes longer to cook. Look through the oven door window if you have one.

• Use lids, whenever possible, to keep in heat and speed up cooking times.

• Try to match the size of the pot to the size of the burner (or the size of the flame) in order not to waste any heat. For instance, put a six-inch pot on a six-inch burner instead of an eight-inch burner.

• Save heat and water by running the dishwasher only when it is full.

• Cook as many dishes at once as possible. Keep the oven at 350° F. If a recipe calls for a higher or lower temperature simply adjust the cooking time instead of the temperature.

• Clean your refrigerator coil at least once a year; that will keep your refrigerator from working too hard and wasting energy.

• If you're planning on leaving town for a week or more, save energy by turning off the refrigerator and freezer (of course, be sure to empty it so food does not spoil).

• Make sure your freezer is packed tightly. If the compartment is not full, add extra bags to fill it.

• Your refrigerator should not be set below 38° F, your freezer below 5° F. Setting it below these temperatures wastes energy!
See page 101 for additional tips on efficient cooking.

large commercial manufacturers of these products test the cleaners on animals in cruel ways. Most of the commercial cleaning products are also packaged wastefully and come in plastic bottles made from nonrenewable petroleum. If you must buy commercial cleaners, buy powdered detergents since they are more concentrated and require less packaging.

The following is a list of different types of cleaners and their natural, nontoxic alternatives. It is also much less expensive to make your own cleaners.

Bath, Tile, and Tub Cleaners

Although commercial cleaners work well to remove sludge and decay, most contain toxic chemicals and are very polluting.

There are many natural ways to remove unwanted deposits from your bathtubs and toilets that don't contain toxins or corrosives and clean just as effectively. One way to remove soap scum and minerals is to apply baking soda and a little bit of water directly to the infected area. Scrub it with a damp cloth for a new shine. Baking soda is both nonabrasive and highly effective. Another alternative is to use vinegar. It can be applied directly or diluted with a little water (one quarter cup to one gallon water) and scrubbed vigorously. Borax also works well but has abrasive qualities unlike baking soda and vinegar. Borax may scratch more delicate plastics.

Carpet and Rug Cleaners and Deodorizers

Most commercial carpet and rug cleaners, as well as deodorizers, contain many highly toxic ingredients.

Small spills and spots on your carpet can easily be removed with club soda. Fuller's earth works great in removing large spots. Fuller's earth is any fine-grained natural substance which has a high absorptive capability. It is clay-like and crumbles into mud when mixed with water. It can be purchased at many health food and grocery stores. Simply sprinkle it (or cornstarch) on the spot and leave it there for at least fifteen minutes to absorb stains and grease, then wash with a mixture of three parts hot water and one part white vinegar. If this does not work, use a soap-based, nonaerosol rug or upholstery shampoo. Salt works well for ketchup, mustard, mud, and dirt stains on carpeting. After the spill, immediately sprinkle carpet with enough salt to soak up the stain. Wipe up the excess salt with a towel, then vacuum.

To deodorize your carpet, sprinkle about one cup baking soda or cornstarch per medium-size room. Let stand for at least thirty minutes before vacuuming. Another effective deodorizer is to mix two parts cornmeal with one part borax, sprinkle liberally, then let stand at least an hour before vacuuming.

Disinfectants

Commercial disinfectants usually contain many highly toxic chemicals such as ammonia, chlorine, cresol, and phenol, all of which pose serious environmental and health hazards.

Instead of wasting your money and polluting the environment, you can make your own disinfectant. A little baking soda on a damp sponge works well cleaning most surfaces. An open box of baking soda in the refrigerator will deodorize the air inside for up to three months. White vinegar or fresh lemon juice either diluted half and half with water or used full strength works well as a disinfectant. One half cup borax mixed in one gallon hot water also works great as a disinfectant.

Drain Cleaners

Commercial drain cleaners contain lye and hydrochloric and sulfuric acids that can burn skin tissue and are very harmful to children if swallowed. Instead of submitting to such hazards, make your own drain cleaner, or better yet, prevent your drains from clogging up by putting a strainer on them to trap hair and dirt particles. As another preventive measure pour, boiling water down the drain once a week; if the water goes down slowly pour 2 tablespoons of baking soda and one half cup of white vinegar down the drain and cover for 60 seconds. (The chemical reaction should unclog most drains). If this does not work, regular flat plungers work great for sinks and the round ones will unclog most toilets.

Floor and Furniture Polish

Most commercial floor and furniture polish contains a toxic chemical called phenol. It is known to cause cancer in animals and can cause severe skin irritation to humans. The vapors from the floor and furniture keep rising long after the initial use. Fortunately there are many effective nontoxic alternatives. A few simple ones are to mix one tablespoon lemon oil with one pint mineral oil; or blend one cup linseed oil, ½ cup white vinegar, and ½ cup rubbing alcohol. Rubbing in a small amount of toothpaste will remove most water marks on wood surfaces. Water marks on furniture can also be removed by allowing a paste of equal parts of salt and salad oil to sit briefly on the spot before wiping.

Glass and Window Cleaners

Like just about all other commercial cleaners, window and glass cleaners take a serious toll on the environment. Fortunately, there are many safe, easy alternatives to cleaning windows and glass rather than relying on commercial products. Lukewarm water and a squeegee work fine for easy jobs. Add one or two tablespoons of vinegar to a pint of warm water and mix vigorously for tougher jobs. Add one tablespoon of rubbing alcohol to any of your solutions if the glass you are cleaning is cold. To reduce waste, be sure to use a towel or rag rather than something disposable.

Metal Polishes

Metal polishes take a serious toll on the environment. Ingredients include ammonia, ethanol, petroleum distillates, and sulfur compounds, all of which give off toxic fumes.

Just about all metals in your household can be cleaned without harmful, expensive cleaners. If fact, most metals can be freed from rust with a paste of two tablespoons salt and

---

🖋 Here is a list of metals along with simple ways to clean them using nontoxic ingredients.

• Aluminum—clean with a soft cloth dipped in straight lemon juice or white vinegar, or soak overnight in a mixture of vinegar and water, then rub.

• Brass and Copper—apply a paste made out of lemon juice and salt or baking soda and leave on for five minutes. Wash off with warm water and dry with a soft cloth. If copper is tarnished, boil it in a pot of water for several hours with one tablespoon salt and one cup vinegar. After boiling it, wash with soap and water, then rinse and dry.

• Chrome—rub with undiluted vinegar, or rub with a lemon peel, rinse, and polish with a soft cloth.

• Gold—wash in lukewarm soapy water, dry, then polish with a soft chamois cloth.

• Silver—soak for ten to fifteen minutes in one quart warm water, one teaspoon baking soda, one teaspoon salt, and a piece of aluminum foil, then wipe with a soft cloth. Another method that works well is to rub on some toothpaste with a soft cloth or rag and wash it off with warm water.

one tablespoon lemon juice. Simply apply with a dry cloth and rub.

Oven Cleaners

Oven cleaners contain many dangerous ingredients, including aerosols, detergents, and lye, a strong caustic that can scorch and mar human tissue. Direct exposure can cause lung damage and cause blindness if splashed on eyes.

The best prevention against these harmful cleaners is to cook food in proper-sized dishes. Aluminum foil lined on the bottom of the oven is a great way to catch spills. While the spills are still hot, sprinkle salt on them, then clean with a paste made of two tablespoons baking soda in one cup hot water. Use a nonmetallic bristle brush or a steel-wool pad to clean the walls of the oven. (Be sure to pick up leftover steel particles with a magnet.)

Scouring Powder

Most commercial scouring powders contain harsh ingredients such as chlorine, detergents, and talc.

Instead of buying commercial products, make your own solution with a mix of table salt (or baking soda) sprinkled on a sponge moistened with equal parts of water and vinegar. Liquid soap also works well if the surface is sprinkled with dolomite powder and scoured with steel wool. A pinch of sodium perborate works well for safe bleaching. If you must buy a commercial product, buy a chlorine-free brand such as Bon Ami (which is made of feldspar and soap).

Toilet Cleaners

Toilet cleaners contain chlorine and hydrochloric acid, which can burn skin and eyes and cause harm to the environment when it enters the water supply.

Instead of relying on commercial products, use soap and

🍂 Safe Household Cleaning Products

The following inexpensive household products are safe to use and effective for most cleaning needs. Using these basics in the ways described above will save you money and the environment.

Baking soda—can be used as an all-purpose cleaner to remove odors and to polish, and even to clean teeth. Baking soda is mildly abrasive, noncorrosive, and safe to ingest.

Beeswax—is another must to have around the house. Melted beeswax added to mineral oil works great as a natural furniture polish.

Borax—usually found in the laundry section of the supermarket, works great as a mild cleaner and for removing odors and preventing the growth of mold. Be careful, however; it is harmful if swallowed.

Fuller's earth—is a clay powder best used to clean up spills on your carpet and upholstery (it works by absorbing liquids).

Lemon juice—works great either diluted or straight as a cleaner or grease remover. It may need to be mixed with other ingredients depending on the use.

Mineral oil—works great as a wood and furniture polish. This safe and odor-free petroleum oil also works great to clean greasy hands.

Pure soap—is made without additives. Either in bar or flake form, it is a highly effective all-purpose cleaner.

Salt—can be used as an all-around household cleaner. It is safe, effective, and costs 40 to 50 cents for 28 ounces.

Vinegar—is a must to have on your cleaning shelf. Common white vinegar cuts grease, removes odors, and prevents the growth of mold.

borax mixed together. Stubborn rings and lime buildup can
be removed with white vinegar. Baking soda also works well
to clean your toilet bowl. Simply sprinkle some into the
bowl, add a touch of vinegar, and scour with a toilet brush.

Sponges

Sponges don't cross most people's minds as being environmental hazards, but they do pose many problems. The main
ingredient in commercial sponges you buy in the supermarket is polyurethane, which is derived from petroleum. So
when you get down to it, sponges are made from a diminishing natural resource, they are polluting to manufacture,
and they don't degrade in landfills. What's the alternative?
Natural sponges from the ocean are what cross most people's minds, but they too are a diminishing natural resource.
The most ecologically sound sponges are made from wood
pulp cellulose. They are long-lasting, degradable, and very
plentiful.

The sponges are available at most health food stores and
fine grocery stores, as well as bath and supply stores.

2 The Hardware Store

🍃 🍃 🍃 🍃 🍃 🍃 🍃 🍃 🍃 🍃 🍃 🍃

This chapter lists dozens of inexpensive products and tips that will increase the longevity of your house, add value to it, and make living more comfortable and efficient. Most important, these products and tips will help ease our environmental problems and may even pay for themselves in the long run.

Energy-Saving Products

Water Heater Insulator

Insulate your water heater with a prefab blanket. This will save 7–8 percent of the energy you've been using. Make sure not to cover air vents on gas heaters. It can save 1,100 pounds of CO_2 per year for an electric water heater or 220 pounds for gas. The blanket is available at most hardware stores for around $15 and will pay for itself in a matter of months.

✿ Lower Your Water Heaters

Most people set their water heaters at 140° F, much higher than necessary. For every 10 degrees the water heater is turned down, 6 percent of the energy will be saved; 120 degrees is sufficient. If every household in America lowered their regular temperature by 4° F, 380,000 barrels of oil would be saved daily.

Heat Traps

Heat traps will also save heat from being wasted from your water heater. As hot water rises and cold water falls within your water heater a lot of heat escapes through the pipes. If your water heater is not equipped with heat traps, you can buy them at your local hardware store for about $30. They are a one-time investment and will pay for themselves within a year through the energy saved and continue to save you up to $30 a year in the future.

Compact Fluorescent Light Bulbs

Replace all incandescent light bulbs with compact fluorescent bulbs—they are huge energy savers. They last ten times longer then incandescent bulbs and use about one quarter of the energy. For instance, a 60-watt incandescent bulb lasts about 750 hours and consumes about $45 worth of energy. A 15-watt compact fluorescent bulb lasts about 7,500 to 10,000 hours (about five to ten years of normal use) and costs only about $10 worth of energy for each period of time that an incandescent bulb burns. By replacing a standard lightbulb with a compact fluorescent bulb, you will save the energy equivalent of 600 pounds of coal over the life of the bulb.

Compact fluorescents cost around $15 to $20 initially, but the savings of $35 per bulb makes the purchase a sound

---

🍃 Lease a Light?

The Municipal Lighting Plant of Taunton, MA, started a program that leases compact fluorescent bulbs to customers. The program, Smartlight, leases bulbs for 20 cents a month and promises customers that they'll save more than $50 over the life of each lamp. The bulbs last approximately five years if burned an average of six hours a day.

---

investment for your wallet and the environment. This does not include the replacement costs of ten incandescent bulbs (about $1.00 each) for the five to ten years that the compact fluorescent bulb lasts. If everyone in America switched from incandescent bulbs to fluorescent, approximately $11 billion would be saved on utility bills alone.

Although compact fluorescent light bulbs are smart choices in most circumstances, they cannot be used with dimmers and do not fit in every light socket. Make sure they are the right size for your socket and can be used for your needs before purchasing them.

Halogen Lighting
Halogen lights are another great way to save energy and landfill space. They work better than compact fluorescents for precise lighting, like for reading or working, and last much longer than incandescent lights. A typical 50-watt halogen light bulb costs about $4 and will last 2,400 hours, more than three times longer than a 50-watt incandescent.

Light Timers
One way to make sure you don't accidentally leave lights on during the day is to put them on a timer or photocell unit, which automatically turns lights off when the sun comes up. A timer runs between $5 and $15 at the hardware store

and will probably pay for itself within a year. If you're the forgetful type, it will pay for itself much sooner.

Watt Watchers

The Watt Watcher is an automatic wall switch that turns off lights when you leave the room. Another type works as a light-sensing control that turns off lights when enough natural lighting enters the room. They cost about $30 and will pay for themselves very quickly, thus saving you money every year on your utility bills.

✿ Tips to Conserve Lighting Energy in Your Home

—Turn off lights in all rooms not being used.

—Concentrate your lighting in reading or working areas and where it is needed for safety.

—Reduce overall lighting in places where it is not necessary. For instance, remove one bulb out of three in multiple light fixtures and replace it with a burned out bulb so that the wires aren't exposed and the danger of electrocution is removed.

—In areas where bright light is needed, use one large bulb instead of several small ones.

—Open your blinds and use natural lighting whenever possible. A three-by-five foot window lets in more light than 100 standard 60-watt bulbs.

—Light-colored walls, draperies, and upholstery reflect more light, therefore requiring less artificial light.

—Turn off all decorative outside gas lamps unless they are essential for safety. You can save between $40 and $50 a year in natural gas costs for every gas lamp you turn off.

—Regularly dust bulbs to get rid of light-absorbing dirt.

Draft Blockers

Instead of losing heat or air conditioning through electrical outlets and light switches, invest in a set of draft blockers. These foam plates fit behind light switches and outlets to reduce drafts. They're easy to install and a packet of ten costs only around $3 at your local hardware store.

Door Sweeps

Installing a door sweep at the bottom of exterior doors will greatly decrease escaping heat or air conditioning. They are available at most hardware stores for about $2–$3 and can pay for themselves in a matter of days.

Caulking/Weather Stripping

To test doors or windows for costly drafts, move a lighted candle around the frames and sashes. If the flame flickers there is probably a leak, and you should caulk or weatherstrip the gaps. The materials for a typical twelve-window, two-door home cost approximately $25, but the savings in energy bills will amount to about 10 percent off your annual costs, hence the materials will pay for themselves in no time.

AFM Enterprises, Inc. (1140 Stacy Court, Riverside, CA, 92507; (714) 781-6860) makes caulking and spackling compounds that are nontoxic.

Curtains and Blinds

An easy way to insulate windows to reduce heat loss is to use thick curtains and make sure they're snugged in tight at night. The sun's heat will warm your home during the day and the curtains will keep the heat in at night. If used correctly, curtains and blinds can reduce heat loss through windows as much as 50 percent and save you an average of $15 per window each winter. Drapes and blinds can also be used in the summer to prevent unwanted heat from the sun.

Storm Doors and Windows

Combination screen and storm doors and windows are a great way to weatherize your home. They act as an additional insulator to keep cool air out and warm air in during the winter, and cool your home during the summer. Annual savings on storm doors and windows can add up to 15 percent a year, so they pay for themselves during a long winter.

Shrink Wrap Plastic Storm Windows

Another great way to insulate windows is to use a commercial shrink wrap plastic seal over your windows. It is easy to install (with an adhesive or with a hair dryer), and can be used year after year if taken down very carefully. A quality product runs about $10 and, like most of the other products in this chapter, will pay for itself very quickly in the decreased use of energy.

Radiator Reflectors

Radiator reflectors are heat-reflecting panels made from insulating material with one face covered by metal foil. They cost only about $5 each and make any radiator more efficient, so they can pay for themselves within a few months. To save even more money, you can make one yourself by cutting a piece of insulation board and taping aluminum foil to the side facing the room.

Radiator Vent

If you heat your home with a radiator, then a radiator vent is a must. Although the valves to regulate heat flow in a radiator can be turned down, they cannot be turned off when heat is not needed. A radiator vent allows you to completely shut off your valves to stop air flow when you are gone for the day or simply don't want heat pouring in. An adjustable radiator vent costs about $10 to $15 and will pay for itself through lower energy bills in no time. It is also easy to install: Simply unscrew the old vent and screw on the new and improved one.

Programmable Thermostats

A programmable thermostat lets you adjust the heating and cooling of your home at certain times. You can program it to have a cool home when you get back from your weekend getaway or make sure your room is toasty when you wake up in the morning. Better yet, you can make sure the heat isn't blasting while you're away at work, saving you

---

✒ Tips on Keeping Warm and Saving Energy

—Cover air conditioners in winter to stop energy loss.

—Close off unused space in your home. This will reduce unnecessary heat use and therefore save energy. Be sure to turn off heaters/coolers and block vents in the closed area.

—Remove radiator covers during the heating season to increase heating efficiency.

—Unless you have a fire burning, keep your fireplace dampers closed during the winter.

—Dress in warmer clothes indoors so you don't have to crank the heat as high.

—Pull down blinds and shades at night to further insulate your house.

—Lower your thermostat. If you set your thermostat back by 10° F. over an eight-hour period, a savings of 9 percent to 18 percent is possible.

—Change or clean furnace filters regularly. Dirty or clogged furnace filters will cause your heaters to work harder and therefore consume more fuel.

> ✿ Tips to Keeping Cool and Saving Energy
>
> —Keep blinds and curtains down during the day to keep out sunlight.
>
> —Keep your air-conditioner filters and coils clean to make it run more efficiently.
>
> —If you live in a warm climate, plant shade trees around windows that receive lots of sunshine. They will greatly cut down on your air-conditioning costs.
>
> —Install fans around your home. They use one-tenth the amount of energy needed by air conditioners and keep you feeling cool.
>
> —When there is a breeze outside, open up the bottom windows at one side of your house and the upper windows on the other side to set up crosscurrents of cool air.

money in the long run by cutting wasted energy. They cost about $40 to $60 and will save you about 20 percent a year if used properly, paying for themselves in less than a year.

Thermostat Outlet

This device is similar to a programmable thermostat but turns an outlet on. It is great for space heaters, especially if used to heat a small portion of a home such as a boxed-in area in your basement to keep your pipes from freezing. They run about $20 to $30 and will pay for themselves in the long run by cutting back on energy bills.

Heat Tape

If your basement is not heated and frozen pipes are on your worry list, invest in some heat tape rather than trying to keep the whole basement above freezing. It is simply a cord that wraps around your pipes and plugs into an outlet.

Some even give off variable heat along their lengths based on the pipe temperature at each point. They are inexpensive to operate and much cheaper than heating your whole basement, let alone fixing the frozen pipes.

Products to Help You Reduce Toxic Waste

Rechargeable Batteries

One simple way to reduce toxic waste is to use rechargeable batteries instead of alkaline batteries. Although both contain mercury and cadmium, the rechargeable ones last much longer and end up costing much less. In landfills batteries release mercury and cadmium into the soil. In turn, the mercury and cadmium pollute ground water. Batteries that are incinerated release toxic waste into the air.

Although the initial investment is much larger, rechargeables pay for themselves quickly. For instance, four "AA" alkaline batteries cost about $3.35. A "AA" recharger lists for about $10. Add four batteries at $11 and you get a total of $21 to get started. The rechargeable batteries last up to 1,000 recharges and the energy used would cost under $5 for all of the recharges. Now say that you would use the rechargeable batteries up to their limit (not inconceivable for joggers relying on Walkmans). If 400 "AA" alkaline batteries needed to be purchased (rechargeables only last about two-fifths of the time of "AA's") it would cost a total of $335. Recharging the rechargeables 1,000 times for the same battery life would cost only $26 including electricity—a savings of $309!

If wasting money and harming the environment doesn't bother you (you wouldn't be reading this book if it didn't) and you still insist on using alkaline batteries, please make sure to have them recycled. If there is no recycling center in your area, push for one.

Natural Paints

Each year Americans buy more than a half-billion gallons of environmentally harmful paint for their homes and buildings.

Most of this paint is toxic and contains volatile organic compounds (VOCs), which mix with nitrogen oxides (from power plants, refiners, and your car's exhaust) in the air to form ground-level ozone, more familiarly known as smog. Paint also causes serious indoor air pollution that's harmful when inhaled.

Producing paint creates another huge environmental concern. It is primarily made from nonrenewable raw materials such as petroleum and coal-tar oil and requires a tremendous amount of energy and toxic chemicals in the process.

Fortunately there is an environmentally sound alternative in paints. A number of companies are manufacturing "natural" paint products with far less toxic ingredients that are extracted from beeswax, plant waxes, linseed oil, and tree resins rather than petroleum-based solvents.

These paints are considerably more expensive and are limited to earth colors, but from Mother Nature's standpoint they are worth it. If a natural paint doesn't suit your needs, use a water-based (latex) paint instead of an oil-based paint (it contains far fewer VOCs).

"Earth-Friendly" Paint Manufacturers

The following companies claim their paints are low in toxicity, are natural, or are made from natural or organic ingredients. Contact them if you have any questions on their usability or costs.

AFM Enterprises, Inc.
   (1140 Stacy Ct., Riverside, CA 92507; (714) 781-6860)
   This company carries a line of nontoxic water-based paint and other home-repair products such as adhesives, sealers, strippers, etc.

Auro-Sinan Co.
(P.O. Box 857, Davis CA 95617; (916) 753-3104)
   Auro-Sinan offers plant-based organic paints, waxes, and cleansers manufactured in Germany and Austria.

The Glidden Company
   (925 Euclid Ave., Cleveland, OH 44115; (800) 221-4100)

✒ What to Do With Paint Leftovers

Think twice before pouring your leftover paints down the drain or into the ground, which pollutes our environment and usually ends up harming nearby streams and ground-water supplies due to runoff. Well, then, what do you do with your leftovers? Here are some sound alternatives:

—If you have more than a half-gallon of paint left over when you've finished your job, recycle it. You can mix several colors together and end up with a beige or gray color that can make a great primer. (Be careful not to mix oil and water paints together, though.)

—Keep your extra paints well marked and give them to a local organization such as a school, theater group, or parks department. Many towns have a community exchange program once or twice a year. If your community doesn't, start one.

—If you can't find anything else to do with your extra paint, take it to a hazardous waste collection site. Some communities even have a curbside collection during the year to pick up such waste.

—Most important, don't buy in bulk unless you're going to use it all. In other words, don't buy a gallon if you only need to paint the trim of a door.

Glidden manufactures what it calls "the first conventional latex paint available in the U.S. which contains no petroleum-based solvents." The paint is called Glidden 2000, and although it is not claimed to be natural or organic, it doesn't emit any VOCs. The paint is available in ready-mixed flat and semigloss interior latex.

Adhesives

For the most part, commercial adhesives, sealants, and glues are highly toxic and are contributors of hydrocarbon emissions. Always look for 100 percent natural adhesives, sealants, and glues that contain no synthetic chemicals, no petrochemicals, and no hydrocarbons, and that are formaldehyde-free and water-based.

EARTH-FRIENDLY ADHESIVES

It can be hard to find nontoxic adhesives at your local hardware store. It's hard enough to read the ingredients and decipher what's harmful to the environment and what's harmonious. These nontoxic liquid adhesives will make your shopping easier.

—CRAYOLA ART & CRAFT GLUE (water-based; Binney & Smith)
—DURAFIX (formaldehyde-free, water-based; Ross Adhesives)
—ELMER'S CARPENTER GLUE (water-based; Borden, Inc.)
—ELMER'S GLUE ALL (water based; Borden, Inc.)
—ROSS KID'S GLUE (formaldehyde-free, water-based; Ross Adhesives)
—SOBO (water-based; Slomons Group)

Household Insecticides

About 300 million pounds of insecticides are used in American homes every year. Commercial brands are highly toxic and unhealthy, and pose huge threats to our air and water quality. The safest way to control unwanted insects is to do it yourself with simple household goods. The following is a list of insects along with simple, natural ways of getting rid of them.

Ants
- keep your floors and countertops clean with a solution of equal parts of vinegar and water.
- Disperse red chili powder, borax, or dry peppermint where you see the ants coming in.
- plant mint by the front and back door of your home to help keep ants out.
- Shower the ants and their hangout spots with a strong mint tea to keep them away.
- A dash of liquid soap in a bucket of water works great as a home-made repellent. Spray it right on the ants.

Beetles and Weevils (these are the critters hanging out in your grains)
- A couple of bay leaves work well in each receptacle of flour, cereal, and corn meal.
- Before storing your grains, freeze them for at least two days.

Cockroaches
- Bay leaves work as a great deterrent. Put them wherever you see cockroaches.
- Garlic works great as a pest-repellent. Either grow it in your garden to keep harmful bugs away or mix it with a soapy liquid in your blender and spray it around infested areas.

Fleas

- Look for organic spray repellents made from cedar-wood, eucalyptus, and bay leaves. They are safe and effective.

- Dips and sprays containing delimonine gas, which is derived from citrus extracts, are safe and work well for fleas and other pests.

Flies

- The most effective way to keep flies out of your house is to put screens on doors and windows.

- Decorate your room with clusters of cloves to keep flies out.

- Leave crushed orange or lemon skins in rooms with flies; the citrus oil repels flies and other insects.

Houseplant Pests

- A safe, nontoxic way to get rid of insects on your plants is to wash or hand spray the leaves and stems with mild soapy water or with pyrethrin, an ingredient derived from chrysanthemums, marigolds, and other members of the aster family.

- To control mealybugs, white flies, spider mites and scale, spray the leaves with lukewarm soapy water or wipe the pests off with a Q-tip soaked in rubbing alcohol.

Mosquitoes

- The easiest and most effective way to keep mosquitoes out of your home is to keep screens on windows and doors.

- Burning oil of citronella rings is also a great way to keep mosquitoes away.

- Attract birds that feast on mosquitoes to your home by planting garlic, marigolds, and other flowers.

Moths

- Commercial cedar moth repellents work very well. To do it yourself and save some money, buy a piece of cedar for your storage closets or put cedar shavings in light cloth bags.

- An alternative to using repellents is to wash all the clothes you're going to store, then pack them in moth-proof sealed boxes. (Washing kills moth eggs.)

Spiders

- Although most people kill spiders to get rid of them, they are actually beneficial to have around the house. They will not contaminate your food in any way and keep insects away that do. If you must get rid of them, let them go outside in a humane way.

Rodent Control

Commercial poisons to keep rodents out of your home work great to kill mice and rats but they pose serious environmental hazards. Although the poisons do control rodents, they can also harm people, pets, and wildlife. And once the rodents are killed, their contaminated remains are easy targets for other animals to feed on.

Poisoned animals can retreat into cracks in your walls and die. The unsanitary remains will smell up your home and are likely to create health risks. The manufacture of these poisons is the worst part; it spews toxic waste into our air and earth at every stage.

Instead of battling the critters when they enter your house, why not cancel their invitations? Make sure your house is clean of any food particles and there is no easy way for them to enter. Plug up any cracks or holes they might be using as entrances. If you still have a rodent problem, the best control is a cat. However, if that is not an option, trapping pests is the next best way. Live traps are of course the most humane way to capture them but then what do you do? If possible, let the pests go far away from your house. If that means sending your problems elsewhere, as in the city, spring-loaded killing traps may be your best option.

Saving Water

Low-Flush Toilet

If building a new house or replacing old toilets, investigate an "ultra-low-flush" toilet. It uses only ½ to 1½ gallons of pressurized water per flush compared to the 5 to 8 gallons of water a traditional toilet uses.

Faucet Aerator

One of the best water-conserving products is the low-flow faucet aerator that can be attached to water faucets in your home. It reduces water flow by up to 50 percent, without reducing pressure, by mixing air in the water as it is dispensed from your tap. Since normal faucet flow is between three to five gallons of water per minute, the faucet aerator will save the average family of four as much as 480 gallons per month, or nearly 6,000 gallons of water a year. It will save you about $8 a year in energy and water savings and can be purchased for a mere $4 at most hardware and plumbing stores.

Save Toilet Water

To save water with a traditional toilet, place a plastic bottle filled with water in your toilet tank. Be careful, however, not to interfere with the flushing mechanism. Another way to save water is to buy a displacement bag specifically designed to hang inside your toilet tank. These options will save one to two gallons per flush.

The average toilet is flushed 8 times per day, which means a savings of 8 to 16 gallons per toilet each day, 56 to 112 gallons a week, 2,900 to 5,800 gallons a year. If a mere one million people did it we would save 2.9 trillion to 5.8 trillion gallons of pure water a year.

To check leaks in your toilet simply add food coloring to the tank (the part behind the toilet that houses the flushing mechanism). Check the toilet 30 minutes later; if there is any color, there is a leak. A leaking toilet can waste up to 200 gallons of water a day.

❧ How Much Water Does the Typical Family of Four Use Per Day?

Activity	Water Use (Gallons)
Toilet Flushing	100
Showering and Bathing	80
Laundry	35
Dishwashing	15
Bathroom Sink	8
Utility Sink	5
Total	243

3 The Clothing Store

❧ ❧ ❧ ❧ ❧ ❧ ❧ ❧ ❧ ❧ ❧ ❧

Believe it or not, the clothes you buy have a major impact on the environment. This chapter explains all the harms certain fabrics and materials have on the environment and, on the other side of the coin, the earth-friendly products that help clean your clothes. It will even have a section on clothing companies who get a check-plus from Mother Nature herself.

Check the Packaging

One of the biggest environmental threats clothes present on the environment is their packaging. Avoid buying clothes that are overpackaged and let the retailer and manufacturer know your reasoning. How many times have you bought a shirt with a dozen or so pins tacked into it, paper placed between every fold, wrapped in a layer of plastic, and bagged or boxed in dyed cardboard? It's time to realize none of this is necessary and time to express exactly how you feel to those who make and sell these goods.

The Harms and Benefits of Clothing Materials

Nearly all materials that go into the making of your clothes are harmful to the environment in one way or another. Even natural fabrics pose great threats to the environment. Although cotton and wool come from plants and animals, they can be as harmful as synthetics, which are derived primarily from petroleum-based chemicals. Of course, we have to wear clothes—so let's make the right choices for Mother Nature's sake.

Cotton

Even though it comes from plants, cotton is still harmful to the environment. First, cotton plants receive about 50 percent of all the pesticides used in America. Furthermore, much of the pesticides, herbicides, and fertilizers used in conventionally grown cotton can be as petroleum-intensive as nylon. To minimize your environmental impact when buying cotton, make sure it hasn't been bleached, treated with harsh chemicals, or dyed. If you need something colorful, make sure it was dyed with a natural dye. Better yet, try to find cotton products that were organically grown. Some companies are responding to the environmental problems associated with cotton. They are producing cotton using methods that are less energy and chemical intensive. (See sources for environmentally sound clothing manufacturers later in this chapter.) Of all clothing materials used, cotton is still one of the least harmful to the environment.

Wool

Wool's durability and ability to absorb moisture and keep you warm even when wet far outweighs its environmental disadvantages. Although it requires far less processing than cotton, environmentalists argue that it does violate the animal protection issue. (In Colorado and other Western states, where nearly all U.S. wool comes from, ranchers are trying to get sheep predators, such as the puma, coyote, or mountain lion, reclassified as varmints so they can legally shoot or poison them for bothering their sheep.) When buying wool products, choose ones that are easy to wash. Bypass wool clothing that is chemically treated or needs dry cleaning at every washing.

Synthetics

Out of all materials used for clothes, synthetics pose the greatest harm to our environment. Although they are very durable, most synthetic materials are derived entirely from fossil fuels such as petroleum, natural gas, and coal—all nonrenewable resources. Manufacturing synthetic materials creates toxic chemicals and pollutes our air and water. And when it is time to discard them, most are nonrecyclable and nonbiodegradable. When choosing between synthetics and other fabrics, you must weigh your needs. Since synthetics are so durable, they are recommended for outdoor wear, sporting gear, and camping equipment. If the decision is up in the air, always choose natural fabrics; they are far less damaging to the environment.

Furs

Each year in the United States almost 17 million animals die agonizing deaths in traps. An additional 30 million animals are killed on ranches just for the fur industry. These include foxes, mink, ocelots, raccoons, chinchillas, etc. Animal cruelty is, of course, the issue here. The animals that are trapped are usually caught by jaws with steel teeth that lock tight around the animals' limbs. If the animal is fortunate enough to chew its leg off, it may have a chance for survival. Otherwise, it waits in pain until the trapper comes and beats it to death with a club. But how do the trappers know what kind of an animal will step in his trap? They don't. For every animal that can be used for its fur, two animals, known in the industry as trash animals, die unnecessarily. These include dogs, cats, deer, birds, etc., that die "by accident."

Besides animal cruelty, most animals are killed solely for their skins; all other body parts are discarded. This is a tremendously wasteful treatment of animals and the natural resources that support them. Killing these animals also disrupts the natural balance of the ecosystems in which they live.

Wearing animal furs is like wearing a sign on your back saying, "I don't care for the lives of animals or the ecosystems in which they live."

Earth-Friendly Clothing Manufacturers

The following is a list of clothing manufacturers that are environmentally responsible. Several even make clothes out of recycled materials.

Ecosport
(28 S. James St., Hackensack, NJ 07606; (800) 486-4326)

This company, founded by two environmentally concerned parents, creates a sportswear line that uses only natural fibers manufactured without bleaches, dyes, and harmful chemicals. They make everything from T-shirts and sweatshirts to babies' crib sheets and blankets.

Patagonia
(Lost Arrow Corp., P.O. Box 150, Ventura, CA 93002;
(805) 643-8616)

Patagonia admits that every piece of clothing has a negative impact on the environment. They encourage their customers to buy only what they need and promise to provide them with the longest-lasting merchandise with minimum waste. Patagonia even has a line of synthetic clothes made from recycled plastic bottles. It is called PCR (post consumer recycled) Synchilla Fleece, and contains 80 percent recycled material and 20 percent virgin polyester. This responsible company has an "Environmental Review Process" to examine the materials and methods used in the production of its merchandise. Patagonia donates ten percent of its profits to environmental organizations.

Buy Recycled Clothes

Buying secondhand clothes is an obvious savings of money and resources. Just about every community has a "nearly new" shop or clothing exchange. These secondhand stores usually have quite nice things that are very inexpensive. You may even bump into brand new clothes that were never worn or your new favorite pair of faded Levis.

Cleaning Your Clothes

Detergents

Commercial laundry and dishwashing detergents pose many threats to our environment. Many of their ingredients, such as phosphates and other cleaning agents, disrupt water ecology and pollute our lakes, streams, and rivers.

🌿 Recycle Your Clothes!

Clothing is one of the most highly overlooked recyclable items. People don't realize the energy and packaging required to manufacture clothing. It is a sad thought that people still send old garments to landfills while there are millions of Americans who can't afford clothes. Nearly every community has at least one organization that will pick up used clothing and distribute it to those in need. In most circumstances, donating old clothes is also tax-deductable.

The most important thing to remember when shopping for detergents is to buy no- or low-phosphate formulas with few harsh ingredients. Also look for companies that do not test on animals, since many large detergent manufactures are known for their inhumane practices (see Chapter 8). And buy the biggest size possible in a container that can be recycled in your area.

Instead of using harsh commercial laundry detergents that contain artificial chemicals and arc nonbiodcgradable, you can substitute them with natural, biodegradable, homemade formulas. Add ⅓ cup washing soda to water before adding dirty clothes to the machine and substitute pure soap flakes or powder for commercial detergents. For extra dirty clothes, add ½ cup borax with the soap or presoak the clothes for thirty minutes with ½ cup washing soda and scrub dirty spots with soap. When switching from a detergent to a soap laundry cleaner for the first time, wash items once with washing soda only. Otherwise, the detergent might react with the soap and cause a yellowing of the fabric.

Bleach
Instead of using a commercial bleach which contains chlorine, add ½ cup borax per washload to whiten whites and brighten colors. If you must buy commercial bleach, buy it without chlorine.

Fabric Softener
To make your own fabric softener, add one cup vinegar or ¼ cup baking soda during final rinse.

The following companies make or sell cruelty-free detergents with ingredients that aren't harsh to the environment. They can be found at your local supermarket or natural food store or can be ordered directly from the company.

—ALLENS NATURALLY, (313) 453-5410.

—ECOVER, order from Mercantile Food Company, (203) 544-9891.

—PROFESSIONAL, order from A Clear Alternative, (713) 356-7031.

—SEVENTH GENERATION, (800) 456-1177.

Shoe Polishes

Commercial shoe polishes contain many toxic substances, all of which are harmful to the environment. Try any one of these natural alternatives and save some money while you're at it.

Olive oil works great on leather shoes of any color; just apply it and buff shine with a soft cloth. Lemon juice works well on black or tan leather shoes; buff to a shine afterwards with a soft cloth. For black suede shoes, apply cool black coffee with a sponge. For patent leather, apply white vinegar with a soft moistened cloth. (Be sure to test for color changes on an inconspicuous section.)

4 The Automotive Shop

Since cars are one of the biggest polluters in America today, this chapter is one of the most essential. It informs you of environmentally safe products for your automobile and earth-friendly alternatives to consider when you are in the market for a new car. You will even take care of and drive your car in a whole new light after reading this chapter. It gives a complete listing of the most fuel-efficient cars for their class and size and the longest-lasting tires. Most important, it informs you of how driving and caring for your car affects the environment.

What to Look for in an Environmentally "Sound" Car

- Buy the most fuel-efficient car possible, one that gets the highest miles-per-gallon among cars in its class and size.
- Choose components that enhance fuel efficiency, such as radial tires and fuel injection.

- Select a car with durable construction and other durable features. It should have long-lasting parts instead of disposables, such as fuel filters and spark plugs.

- Be certain it uses nontoxic and nonpolluting fluids and systems—for instance, non-CFC air-conditioning coolants and nontoxic antifreeze.

- Make sure it's manufactured in the most environmentally friendly ways possible—such as having low-emissions paints and finishes.

- Find out if the manufacturer has a good environmental record in relation to other car manufacturers.

Don't Buy Too Much of a Car

If you're basically going to be running around town with a friend or two and a few bags of groceries, buy a small car with a small engine. This will save you money on gas, the car itself, its maintenance, and insurance. And even better, a small automobile will do less damage to the environment.

Pass up the Power Gadgets

Let's not be lazy. Is it really that hard to roll up the windows or move your seat by hand? All these power gadgets really do is consume more gas and cost more to get fixed.

✖ Don't Buy a Guzzler

A car that gets 40 miles per gallon compared to one that gets 25 miles per gallon and is driven 20,000 miles a year will cut your annual CO_2 emissions by 6,600 pounds a year. This will also reduce your gasoline costs.

Cruise Control

Cruise control is one gadget that may be worth considering. For one thing, it makes highway driving more comfortable. The automatic mechanism in cruise control also controls speeds more efficiently than most drivers and thus helps you save gas.

Turbo

Power boosters for cars are not recommended unless you are a racecar driver. They typically cost more off the bat, waste gas, break down easily, and are expensive to repair.

What Color to Buy?

Believe it or not, the color you choose is important, since dark colors absorb heat and light colors reflect heat. Simply put, if you live in a warm climate buy a light-colored car. This will require you to use less air conditioning, and thus will save gas. Even if it gets cold in the winter, it's still worth it since heat is basically free. It comes directly from the heat your car's engine emits, so it exists whether you use it or not. This goes for the interior of your car as well. Dark upholstery retains heat longer, therefore requiring more air conditioning to cool it down. Of course, the opposite is true if you live in a very cold climate: buy a dark-colored car. (And when deciding what kind of upholstery to get, keep in mind that cloth upholstery and seat covers don't heat up as fast as plastic and thus save air conditioning.)

High-Octane Gasoline

An astonishing 40 percent of drivers buy a high-octane gasoline while only about 10 percent of cars made since 1982 require it. A higher octane's sole purpose is to reduce engine knocking. The cars that do require the highest-octane gasoline are cars with high-compression engines like Jaguars, BMWs and Porsches. As for the rest of us, don't be fooled by the advertisements that the oil companies spend million of dollars on. They just want you to spend an extra 25 cents a gallon for something you don't need.

The worst part about higher-octane gasoline is that it is more harmful to the environment. "Aromatics," a category of hydrocarbons, are added to boost the octane level. The most common aromatics are benzene, toluene, and xylene, which are all big pollutants.

Tires

Every year, Americans "throw away" about 250 million tires.

Now think of that startling statistic in light of the fact that they don't decompose. Each year, tires take up an estimated ½ million cubic yards of landfill space in New York State alone.

What can we do about the tire problem? The best solution is not to drive or own a car. But more realistically, you should concentrate on minimizing the number of tires you go through.

Getting the most life out of your tires isn't just economically sound. By maintaining them properly, you will conserve the energy and resources it takes to manufacture them, save gasoline, cut down on the pollution rates generated by tire production, and save landfill space. And you'll save money!

Unfortunately, most tires wear out 40,000 miles shy of their life span (80,000 to 100,000 miles). In order to get the most out of your tires you must keep them properly inflated, balanced, and rotated every 6–8,000 miles.

It's hard to fathom your tires' inflation having anything

to do with the rise in pollution, but it does. Underinflation wastes up to five percent of your car's gas mileage by increasing the rolling resistance. It also shortens the life of your tires, thus adding to landfill space and tire production at a faster rate.

After getting the most miles out of the life of your tires, take them to a recycling center that accepts them. The recycled rubber will be used for more tires, adhesives, wire and pipe insulation, hoses, sporting goods, and many other products. The energy required to make recycled rubber products is about 71 percent less than that for producing them out of virgin rubber.

PRODUCTS MADE FROM TIRES

Of the growing number of companies that are becoming environmentally conscious, these manufacture products made out of recycled tires.

—CARLISLE TIRE AND RUBBER (Box 99, Carlisle, PA 17013; (800) 233-7165) makes interlocking floor tiles out of recycled tires.

—DEJA SHOE (7180 SW Firloop, Tigard, OR 97233; (503) 624-7443) makes footwear from recycled materials. Some of their shoe soles are made from 100 percent recycled tires.

—U-SAVE TIRE RECYCLERS (3 Craigie Circle, Cambridge, MA 02138, (617) 864-2189) manufactures a child's handcrafted tire swing made from recycled tire rubber.

—TRIO INDUSTRIES (918 Canton St., Box 333, Prescott, WI 54021; (800) 288-3499) makes exercise mats out of recycled tires.

Buy Retreaded Tires

To reduce the amount of tires sent to the landfill, buy retreaded tires whenever possible. Be sure to buy them from a reputable source; poorly made retreaded tires can be hazardous. They are available at most tire stores, auto parts shops, or auto service centers. Be aware, however; the salesperson may try to sell you a new tire rather than a retreaded one. (They make more money on new ones.)

Air Conditioning Saves Gas

When traveling at high speeds, a car with its air conditioning on gets better gas mileage than one with its windows down and no air conditioning. Open windows create a lot of drag, forcing your engine to work harder to keep up the car's speed.

✖ Increase the Efficiency of Your Car

Believe it or not, the way you drive your car greatly affects the amount of gas you emit into the atmosphere. Here are some suggestions to help reduce your car's fuel consumption:

—Instead of warming your engine before driving, start off driving slowly.

—Avoid racing your engine.

—Turn off your engine if you have to idle for more than one minute; you are getting zero miles per gallon while idling.

—Accelerate and slow down gently; avoid quick starts and quick braking unless necessary.

—Follow speed limits; your car's fuel efficiency drops greatly at high speeds.

—Avoid short trips; city driving consumes twice as much fuel as highway driving.

—To increase your car's gas efficiency, get tune-ups regularly and change both air and oil filters often.

—Don't ride your brake. It wastes gas and wears down your brake pads and shoes prematurely. If you know you are coming to a stop, take your foot off the gas and coast to it rather than applying the brake and wasting gas.

—Avoid tailgating. It requires too much braking and accelerating, and thus wastes gas.

—Avoid driving in peak times. It is a great waste of gas and time driving in touch-and-go traffic.

—If your household has more than one car, use the most efficient one around town. This will save gas and make parking easier (it is probably the smaller of the two).

Recycle Your Oil

Recycling used motor oil is more than just saving natural resources. If not properly disposed of, used motor oil is extremely harmful to the environment. A single quart of used motor oil can pollute 250,000 gallons of drinking water. Just one pint can cause a poisonous oil slick one acre in diameter, and Americans dispose of 350 million gallons of used motor oil each year, the equivalent of three Exxon Valdez oil spills every month.

Discarding your motor oil in the trash is the same as pouring it on the ground or down the sewer. It will end up in a landfill and eventually seep into the ground, polluting ground water and drinking water. And unfortunately, about half of all motorists change their oil themselves and 90 percent of them either dump their used motor oil down the drain or into the trash.

What *should* you do with used motor oil? If you change your oil yourself make sure to put it in a safe container and recycle it at your nearby gas station or oil changing outlet. *Do the same with antifreeze/coolant.* Be sure to drain your oil filter into the container (for up to 24 hours) since a used oil filter contains about a quart of oil. Also, don't contaminate the oil with anything else or it could ruin the oil and make it nonrecyclable. Sometimes there is a small fee ranging from 25 cents to 1 dollar per quart. If you take your car to a gas station or quick oil-changing outlet make sure they recycle your oil.

Use Recycled Oil

Although most people aren't aware recycled oil exists, it is available and as good if not better than the original virgin oil. If everyone switched to recycled motor oil we would keep millions of gallons of toxic waste out of our environment every year and reduce oil consumption. Many quick oil-change shops carry recycled oil; if they don't, find one that does and tell the other one your reason for going elsewhere. If you change your oil yourself, many auto parts stores carry recycled motor oil.

Energy-Conserving Oil

If you do use traditional "virgin" motor oil, look for the words "Energy Conserving II" on the container's label. This type of oil contains special additives that help reduce friction and increase your car's gas mileage. According to the American Petroleum Institute, "Energy Conserving II" gets two to three percent better fuel efficiency than standard oil.

Reusable Oil Filters

If you're really serious about saving the environment, invest in a permanent oil filter. The filter retails for about $100, a little more than disposables which cost about $5, but last up to 100 oil changes and can be detached and installed on another car. They will help keep the nearly 400 million oil filters out of our depleting landfills and save you money in the long run.

✍ Cut Down on Driving

—One of the best ways to cut down on your driving is to plan trips mindfully. That is, choose the shortest noncongested route possible.

—If possible, always use your town's public transportation. Buses and subways can be even quicker than driving your car and searching for a parking space. And for every 1,000 people riding to work by bus or rail rather than driving, it saves the environment about 5 tons of hydrocarbons, about 31 tons of carbon monoxide, and about 2.5 tons of nitrogen oxides.

—Join a carpool if public transportation isn't an option. You will save gas money and reduce wear and tear on your car. To join or start a carpool look in the index of your yellow pages or go to the local community center. Some cities even have computer networks of commuters who carpool to work, listed by area.

—Bicycling is by far the best means of transportation. It is environmentally friendly and is a great form of exercise. In some congested areas it can even be quicker than driving a car. Encourage your workplace to make biking to work simple instead of a chore. Request showers, sturdy bike racks, and changing facilities. Some companies even give incentives to employees who bike to work.

—Encourage your community to be more bicycle-friendly. Ask for special bike lanes and make sure they keep the roadsides clear of obstacles. All this can usually be done without straining your town's budget too much.

Recycle Your Car Batteries

Automobile batteries pose a serious threat to our environment. Over eighty million lead-acid batteries are discarded every year. Of these, about 80 percent are recycled. But the remaining 20 percent, or 16 million, end up leaking toxic substances into landfills every year.

Take your used car battery to a service station, reclamation center, or household hazardous-waste collection center as soon as you need to dispose of it. Don't let it sit around your house for long; car batteries can be a fire hazard.

Rebuild Your Engine
Rather than junking your car when the engine goes, rebuild the engine to make it last another 50,000 or so miles. Every year, around nine million cars are taken to the junk yard, which wastes the equivalent of ten billion tons of resources (including steel, glass, etc.) and an unbelievable amount of energy used to produce them. So why add to the problem when you can keep your car running longer and save money by not buying a new one?

Park in the Shade
It is a smart move to park in the shade on hot, sunny days. This will decrease the amount of air conditioning needed and keep hot gas vapors from evaporating.

✄ Extend the Life of Your Car

Though today's cars don't require the maintenance of their predecessors, they still require a certain amount of tender loving care to keep them running longer. The following is a general schedule of maintenance checks and procedures, listed chronologically as they should occur. Most of them you can perform yourself, but if in doubt it is worth the extra money to get it done correctly by a trained mechanic. Remember, this is only a general list. Check your owner's manual for the exact care for your kind of car (failing to do so could void your car's warranty). Keeping your car running efficiently will cut down on the amount of gas consumed (as much as 10 percent), keep your car out of the repair shop, and extend the life of your car, thus keeping it out of the landfill prematurely.

Every Week
—Check oil level

—Check tire pressure (including spare)

—Check window-washing fluid

—Inspect headlamps, taillights, turn signals, windshield wipers, etc.

—Check battery fluid level once a week during the summer (once a month during cooler months), and clean terminals as necessary.

Every Month
—Check coolant level

—Inspect radiator hoses for cracks, leaks, or bulges

—Check air filter for accumulated dirt

—Check belts for looseness or cracking

—Inspect battery terminals for erosion

—Check air conditioning system

Every 3,000 Miles (or three months)
—Change oil and filter

—Inspect exhaust system

—Examine front suspension

—Check power-steering fluid level

—Inspect brake-fluid level

—Examine transmission-fluid level (automatic) or inspect clutch

—Check differential-gear and rear-axle fluid (if applicable)

Once a Year
—Inspect brake system

—Examine fuel-injection system (or carburetor), hoses, and emissions control systems

—Rotate and check alignment and balance of tires

—Lubricate chassis

—Perform tune-up

—Lubricate hood, trunk, and door hinges, as well as outside locks

Every Other Year
—Change oil filter

—Flush cooling system

—Change automatic-transmission fluid and filter, adjust bands
(Source: *Consumer Digest*, September/October 1993.)

Cold Starts—High Pollution

The average automobile trip in the United States is about nine miles. Unfortunately, these short trips are the most detrimental. When your car's engine is cold, it requires a much higher ratio of gasoline to air to operate. Gas also needs to heat up and turn into vapor for it to work in an engine, so when your engine is cold, gas doesn't heat up as easily and much of it ends up pouring out the tailpipe as a liquid.

The engine isn't the only thing that doesn't work efficiently when cold. Your catalytic converter, the device that turns your car's pollutants into carbon dioxide, water, and nitrogen, also needs to heat up before working. So when you first start your car, all the harmful pollutants cough out of your tailpipe before the catalytic converter heats up.

During a typical twenty-mile drive, half of the hydrocarbons (pollutants) are emitted during the first three or four miles. Reducing short trips and cold starts will increase gas mileage and decrease pollution. Avoid them whenever possible.

Engine Heaters

If you live in an extremely cold area an engine heater is a great investment. This device keeps your engine and other components "preheated" so they are ready to go in the morning without wasting time and polluting the atmosphere with toxins. It does, of course, have to be plugged in, but the energy consumed is nothing compared to the emissions saved. Some new cars have outlets built into their engines, but installing one is very easy. The cost is as little as $20, and a heater could pay for itself very quickly with the gas saved.

Don't Top Off the Tank

Unfortunately, many people add a little more gas after the automatic gas pump turns off. (Don't you think the gas station would want to sell you the extra gas in the first place?) When you drive, gas is heated and turns into vapors, hence it expands. Topping off your tank only sends this unneeded gas into the atmosphere.

Vapor Trapping Devices

If possible, always go to a gas station with vapor trapping devices on the pump handles. It is much less polluting and just as easy to use. If your local gas station doesn't have the devices, switch stations and tell them your reasons.

Although they know the earth-saving benefits, many stations have neglected to buy these devices because they cost several hundred dollars each.

Carpool

According to the Union of Concerned Scientists, over 80 percent of all car commuter trips in the United States have only one person in the car—the driver. The best way to help cut down the over 200 million gallons of gasoline Americans consume in their automobiles every day is to carpool, or have a packed car wherever you go. This will reduce the amount of cars on the road and thus will reduce traffic. Carpooling also cuts down on the amount of wear and tear on cars left at home, which will in turn help them last longer.

Cleaning Your Car

Most commercial cleaners for your automobile contain many toxic ingredients that aren't at all necessary. The following is a list of natural nontoxic alternatives to clean your car.

- Air Freshener: To absorb chemical odors, place two or three bags of Odor-Fresh Zeolite in your car.
- Chrome: Simply rub with undiluted vinegar or rub it with a lemon peel, rinse and polish with a soft cloth. Another method is to use ¼ cup baking soda and enough water to make a paste. Apply the paste with a sponge and rub the chrome.
- Leather: Put ½ cup food-grade linseed oil with ½ cup vinegar and a few drops of liquid vitamin E into a jar and shake well. Rub it into the leather with a soft cloth but be sure to test it on a discrete area first.

- Rust Protection: Food-grade linseed oil works well to protect a car from road salt. Simply polish your car with a soft cloth rag saturated in linseed oil.

- Vinyl: Simply mix one teaspoon to ¼ cup washing soda and one cup boiling water together until the washing soda has completely dissolved. Wipe the mixture on the vinyl with a sponge and, if needed, rinse afterwards. (The more washing soda used, the more rinsing needed.)

CLEAN COMMERCIAL CAR CLEANERS

Some companies are starting to recognize the problems associated with the chemicals in their products. The following companies make automotive cleaners with minimal environmental risks. They lack or minimize the volatile organic compounds (VOCs), chlorofluorocarbons (CFCs), and nonbiodegradable substances commercial cleaners of the past consisted of.

—THE LOCTITE CORPORATION makes a line called Permatex Enviro-Safe. These aerosol cleaners include a cleaner/ degreaser, brake and auto parts cleaner, and a carb and choke cleaner. The products meet four of the company's most important objectives in making earth-friendly products: biodegradability, low toxicity, non-flammability, and a lack of CFCs. These cleaners are available at auto parts stores.

—BLUE CORAL has a line called Mechanics Brand Pro-Earth consisting of cleaners such as an engine degreaser, brake cleaner, and carb cleaner. All of the products are biodegradable and contain no chlorinated solvents or CFCs. These cleaners may be ordered through Blue Coral, 1215 Valley Belt Rd., Cleveland, Ohio 44131, telephone (800) 321-8577.

MODEL YEAR 1995 FUEL ECONOMY GUIDE
EPA FUEL ECONOMY ESTIMATES
OCTOBER 1994

United States Department of Energy

KEY

Transmission Types		Codes	
A	AUTOMATIC	D	DIESEL
L	AUTOMATIC LOCKUP	T	TURBO
M	MANUAL	G	GUZZLER TAX
#	3-SPEED, 4-SPEED, ETC.	P	USES PREMIUM
			UNLEADED FUEL

CITY/HWY: MILES PER GALLON FOR CITY AND HIGHWAY DRIVING

ENG/CYL: ENGINE SIZE IN LITERS, AND NUMBER OF CYLINDERS

Two Seaters

	TRANS	CITY/HWY		ENG/CYL	CODE
CHEVROLET CORVETTE	M6	17	25	5.70/8	P
DODGE VIPER	M6	12	21	8.0/10	GP
FERRARI F355 BERLINETTA/G.	M6	10	15	3.5/8	GP
F512M	M5	11	16	4.9/12	GP
348 TB/TS/SPIDER	M5	12	19	3.4/8	GP
HONDA CIVIC DEL SOL	L4	29	36	1.5/4	
LAMBORGHINI					
DB132/DIABLO	M5	9	14	5.7/12	GP
MAZDA MX-5 MIATA	L4	22	28	1.8/4	
RX-7	L4	17	24	1.3/2	TP
MERCEDES-BENZ SL320	A5	17	24	3.2/6	P
SL500	A4	16	21	5.0/8	GP
SL600	A4	13	18	6.0/12	GP
NISSAN 300ZX	L4	18	23	3.0/6	P

	Trans	City/Hwy		Eng/Cyl	Code
PORSCHE 968	A4	17	25	3.0/4	P
TOYOTA MR2	M5	20	27	2.0/4	TP

Minicompact Cars

AUDI Cabriolet	L4	18	26	2.8/6	P
BMW 318i Convertible	L4	21	29	1.8/4	P
325i Convertible	L4	20	28	2.5/6	P
MERCEDES E320	A4	18	23	3.2/6	P
NISSAN 240SX	L4	21	26	2.4/4	P
PORSCHE 911					
Carrera 4/2	A4	17	24	3.6/6	P
928 GTS	L4	15	19	5.4/8	GP
968	A4	17	25	3.0/4	P
TOYOTA Celica					
Convertible	L4	22	29	2.2/4	
Paseo	L4	26	33	1.5/4	
Supra	L4	18	24	3.0/6	P

Subcompact Cars

ACURA Integra	M5	25	31	1.8/4	P
BMW M3	L5	19	28	3.0/6	P
318i, 318iS	L4	21	29	1.8/4	P
325i, 325iS	L4	20	28	2.5/6	P
840Ci	L5	16	24	4.0/8	GP
CHEVROLET Camaro	L4	19	28	3.40/6	
CHRYSLER LaBaron					
Convertible	L4	20	29	3.0/6	
DODGE Stealth	L4	18	24	3.0/6	
EAGLE Summit	A3	28	32	1.5/4	
Talon	L4	22	31	2.0/4	
FERRARI 456 GT	M6	10	16	5.5/12	GP
FORD Aspire	L3	29	34	1.3/4	

	Trans	City/Hwy		Eng/Cyl	Code
Mustang	L4	19	29	3.8/6	
Probe	L4	22	31	2.0/4	
GEO Metro	M5	44	49	10.3	
HONDA Civic	L4	29	36	1.5/4	
Civic HB VX	M5	44	51	1.5/4	
Prelude	L4	23	28	2.2/4	
HYUNDAI SCoupe	L4	25	34	1.5/4	
INFINITI J30	L4	18	23	3.0/6	P
JAGUAR XJS Convertible	L4	17	24	4.0/6	P
XJS Coupe	L4	17	24	4.0/6	P
XJS V12 Convertible	L4	12	16	6.0/12	GP
XJS V12 Coupe	L4	12	17	6.0/12	GP
LEXUS SC300/SC400	L4	18	23	3.0/6	P
MAZDA MX-3	L4	25	34	1.6/4	
MX-6	L4	23	31	2.0/4	
MERCEDES-BENZ E320	A4	20	26	3.2/6	P
MITSUBISHI Eclipse	L4	22	31	2.0/4	
Mirage	A3	28	32	1.5/4	
3000 GT	L4	18	24	3.0/6	
NISSAN Sentra Classic	L4	26	34	1.6/4	
Sentra/200SX	L4	28	37	1.6/4	
300ZX 2+2	L4	18	23	3.0/6	P
PONTIAC Firebird/Formula	L4	19	28	3.40/6	
ROLLS-ROYCE					
Bentley Continental	L4	10	15	6.75/8	GP
Corniche IV	L4	10	15	6.75/8	GP
Corniche S	L4	10	15	6.75/8	TGP
SAAB 900 Convertible	M5	20	27	2.0/4	T
SATURN SC	L4	24	34	1.90/4	
SUBARU Impreza	L4	24	30	1.8/4	
Impreza AWD	L4	22	28	1.8/4	
SVX	L4	17	25	3.3/6	P
SVX AWD	L4	17	25	3.3/6	P

	Trans	City/Hwy		Eng/Cyl	Code
SUZUKI SWIFT	A3	35	38	1.0/3	
TOYOTA CELICA	L4	27	34	1.8/4	
TERCEL	L3	31	35	1.5/4	
VOLKSWAGEN CABRIO	L4	22	28	2.0/4	

Compact Cars

	Trans	City/Hwy		Eng/Cyl	Code
ACURA LEGEND	L4	19	24	3.2/6	P
ALFA ROMEO 164	L4	15	22	3.0/6	GP
AUDI A6	L4	19	24	2.8/6	
A6 QUATTRO	L4	18	22	2.8/6	
S6	M5	18	23	2.2/5	TP
90	L4	18	26	2.8/6	P
90 QUATTRO	M5	19	25	2.8/6	P
BMW 525I	L4	18	25	2.5/6	P
530I	L5	17	26	3.0/8	P
540I	L5	17	25	4.0/8	P
BUICK SKYLARK	L3	22	30	2.30/4	
CHEVROLET BERETTA	L3	25	32	2.20/4	
CAVALIER	L3	25	32	2.20/4	
CORSICA	L3	25	32	2.20/4	
CHRYSLER SEBRING	L4	22	31	2.0/4	
DODGE AVENGER	L4	22	31	2.0/4	
NEON	L3	27	33	2.0/4	
FORD CONTOUR	L4	24	32	2.0/4	
ESCORT	L4	23	29	1.8/4	
GEO PRIZM	L3	26	30	1.6/4	
HONDA ACCORD	L4	23	29	2.2/4	
HYUNDAI ACCENT	L4	28	36	1.5/4	
ELANTRA	M5	22	29	1.6/4	
INFINITI G20	L4	22	28	2.0/4	
JAGUAR XJR	L4	15	21	4.0/6	GP
XJ12	L4	12	16	6.0/12	GP
XJ6	L4	17	23	4.0/6	P

	TRANS	CITY/HWY		ENG/CYL	CODE
KIA SEPHIA	L4	23	31	1.6/4	
LEXUS ES300	L4	20	28	3.0/6	
LINCOLN-MERCURY					
MYSTIQUE	L4	24	32	2.0/4	
TRACER	L4	23	29	1.8/4	
MAZDA MILLENIA	L4	20	28	2.3/6V-6	P
PROTEGE	L4	26	35	1.5/4	
323	L4	26	33	1.6/4	
MERCEDES-BENZ					
C220	A4	23	28	2.2/4	P
C280	A4	20	26	2.8/6	P
E320	A4	20	26	3.2/6	P
E420	A4	18	24	4.2/8	P
S500	A4	15	20	5.0/8	GP
S600	A4	13	17	6.0/12	GP
MITSUBISHI DIAMANTE	L4	18	25	3.0/6	P
NISSAN STANZA ALTIMA	L4	21	29	2.4/4	
OLDSMOBILE ACHIEVA	L3	22	30	2.30/4	
PLYMOUTH NEON	L3	27	33	2.0/4	
PONTIAC GRAND AM	L3	22	30	2.30/4	
SUNFIRE	L3	25	32	2.20/4	
ROLLS-ROYCE					
BENTLEY CONTINENTAL R	L4	10	16	6.75/8	TGP
SATURN SL	L4	24	34	1.90/4	
SUBARU LEGACY	L4	23	31	2.2/4	
LEGACY AWD	L4	22	28	2.2/4	
TOYOTA COROLLA	L3	26	30	1.6/4	
VOLKSWAGEN GOLF III	L4	23	29	2.0/4	
GTI VR6	M5	18	25	2.8/6	
JETTA III	L4	23	29	2.0/4	
JETTA III GLX	L4	18	25	2.8/6	
VOLVO 960	L4	18	24	2.5/6	

	Trans	City/Hwy		Eng/Cyl	Code
Mid-Size Cars					
BMW 740i	L5	16	24	4.0/8	GP
740iL	L5	16	24	4.0/8	GP
BUICK Century	L3	25	32	2.20/4	
Regal	L4	19	29	3.10/6	
Riviera	L4	19	29	3.80/6	
CADILLAC ElDorado	L4	16	25	4.68/8	
CHEVROLET Lumina/					
Monte Carlo	L4	19	29	3.10/6	
CHRYSLER Cirrus	L4	20	29	2.5/6	
DODGE Spirit	L3	22	28	2.5/4	
Stratus	L4	20	29	2.5/6	
FORD Taurus	L4	20	30	3.0/6	
Taurus FFV	L4	19	28	3.0/6	
Thunderbird	L4	19	26	3.8/6	
HYUNDAI Sonata	L4	21	28	2.0/4	
INFINITI Q45	L4	17	22	4.5/8	GP
Q45 full-active					
suspension	L4	15	21	4.5/8	GP
LEXUS GS300	L4	18	23	3.0/6	P
LS400	L4	19	25	4.0/8	P
LINCOLN-MERCURY Cougar	L4	19	26	3.8/6	
Mark VIII	L4	18	25	4.6/8	P
Sable	L4	20	30	3.0/6	
MAZDA 626	L4	23	31	2.0/4	
929	L4	19	24	3.0/6V-6	P
NISSAN Maxima	L4	21	28	3.0/6	
OLDSMOBILE Aurora	L4	17	24	4.00/8	P
Cutlass Ciera	L3	25	32	2.20/4	
Cutlass Supreme	L4	19	29	3.10/6	
PLYMOUTH Acclaim	L3	22	28	2.5/4	
PONTIAC Grand Prix	L4	19	29	3.10/6	

	Trans	City/Hwy		Eng/Cyl	Code
ROLLS-ROYCE					
BENTLEY BROOKLANDS &					
(LWB)	L4	10	15	6.75/8	GP
ROLLS-ROYCE FLYING SPUR	L4	10	16	6.75/8	TGP
SPIRIT III/SPUR III/DAWN	L4	10	15	6.75/8	GP
TURBO R/RL BKLDS/TURBO/					
LW	L4	10	16	6.75/8	TGP
SAAB 900	M5	21	28	2.0/4	T
TOYOTA CAMRY	L4	21	28	2.2/4	
VOLKSWAGEN PASSAT	L4	18	25	2.8/6	
VOLVO 850	L4	19	26	2.3/5	T
940	A4	19	24	2.3/4	T

Large Cars

	Trans	City/Hwy		Eng/Cyl	Code
BUICK LESABRE	L4	19	29	3.80/6	
PARK AVENUE	L4	19	29	3.80/6	
ROADMASTER	L4	17	25	5.70/8	
CADILLAC DEVILLE/					
CONCOURS	L4	16	25	4.60/8	P
FLEETWOOD	L4	17	25	5.70/8	
SEVILLE	L4	16	25	4.60/8	P
CHEVROLET CAPRICE	L4	18	26	4.30/8	
CHRYSLER CONCORDE	L4	20	28	3.3/6	
NEW YORKER/LHS	L4	18	26	3.5/6	
DODGE INTREPID	L4	20	28	3.3/6	
EAGLE VISION	L4	20	28	3.3/6	
FORD CROWN VICTORIA	L4	17	25	4.6/8	
LINCOLN-MERCURY					
GRAND MARQUIS	L4	17	25	4.6/8	
TOWN CAR	L4	17	25	4.6/8	
MERCEDES-BENZ S320	A5	17	24	3.2/6	P
S350	A4	21	28	3.5/6	TD
S420	A4	15	20	4.2/8	GP

	TRANS	CITY/HWY		ENG/CYL	CODE
S500	A4	15	19	5.0/8	GP
S600	A4	13	16	6.0/12	GP
OLDSMOBILE EIGHTY-EIGHT	L4	19	29	3.80/6	
NINETY-EIGHT	L4	19	29	3.80/6	
PONTIAC BONNEVILLE	L4	19	29	3.80/6	
ROLLS-ROYCE BENTLEY					
LIMOUSINE	L4	10	14	6.75/8	GP
SILVER SPUR III LIMOUSINE	L4	10	14	6.75/8	GP
SAAB 9000	A4	18	27	2.3/4	T
TOYOTA AVALON	L4	20	28	3.0/6	

Small Station Wagons

	TRANS	CITY/HWY		ENG/CYL	CODE
AUDI A6 QUATTRO WAGON	L4	18	22	2.8/6	
A6 WAGON	L4	19	23	2/8/6	
BNW 525I TOURING	L4	18	25	2.5/6	P
530I TOURING	L4	17	26	3.0/8	P
FORD ESCORT WAGON	L4	26	34	1.9/4	
HONDA ACCORD WAGON	L4	21	27	2.2/4	
LINCOLN-MERCURY					
TRACER WAGON	L4	26	34	1.9/4	
SATURN SW	L4	24	34	1.90/4	
SUBARU IMPREZA WAGON	L4	23	30	1.8/4	
IMPREZA WAGON AWD	L4	22	29	2.2/4	
TOYOTA COROLLA WAGON	L4	27	34	1.8/4	
VOLVO 960 WAGON	L4	18	24	2.5/6	

Mid-Size Station Wagons

	TRANS	CITY/HWY		ENG/CYL	CODE
BUICK CENTURY WAGON	L3	22	29	2.20/4	
EAGLE SUMMIT WAGON	L4	24	29	1.8/4	
FORD TAURUS WAGON	L4	20	30	3.0/6	
LINCOLN-MERCURY					
SABLE WAGON	L4	20	30	3.0/6	
MERCEDES-BENZ E320	A4	18	24	3.2/6	P

	Trans	City/Hwy		Eng/Cyl	Code
MITSUBISHI Expo	L4	20	26	2.4/4	
Expo. LRV	L4	24	29	1.8/4	
OLDSMOBILE Cutlass					
Cruiser	L4	19	29	3.10/6	
SUBARU Legacy Wagon	L4	23	31	2.2/4	
Legacy Wagon AWD	L4	22	28	2.2/4	
TOYOTA Camry Wagon	L4	21	28	2.2/4	
VOLKSWAGEN					
Passat Wagon	L4	18	25	2.8/6	
VOLVO 850 Wagon	L4	19	26	2.3/5	T
940 Wagon	L4	19	26	2.3/4	

Large Station Wagons

	Trans	City/Hwy		Eng/Cyl	Code
BUICK Roadmaster Wagon	L4	17	25	5.70/8	
CHEVROLET					
Caprice Wagon	L4	17	25	5.70/8	

Small Pickup Trucks/2WD

	Trans	City/Hwy		Eng/Cyl	Code
CHEVROLET S10 Pickup	L4	20	26	2.20/4	
GMC Sonoma	L4	20	26	2.20/4	
ISUZU Pickup	M5	22	25	2.3/4	
MITSUBISHI Truck	L4	19	23	2.4/4	
NISSAN Truck	L4	21	25	2.4/4	

Small Pickup Trucks/4WD

	Trans	City/Hwy		Eng/Cyl	Code
MITSUBISHI Truck	M5	17	22	3.0/6	

Standard Pickup Trucks/2WD

	Trans	City/Hwy		Eng/Cyl	Code
CHEVROLET C1500					
Pickup	L4	16	21	4.30/6	
C2500 Pickup	L4	16	21	4.30/6	
DODGE Dakota Pickup	M5	23	27	2.5/4	

	Trans	City/Hwy		Eng/Cyl	Code
RAM 1500 Pickup	L4	15	19	3.9/6	
RAM 2500 Pickup	L4	13	17	5.2/8	
FORD F150 Pickup	L4	15	20	4.9/6	
F250 Pickup	L4	14	18	4.9/6	
Lightning F150	L4	12	16	5.8/8	
GMC C1500 Sierra	L4	16	21	4.30/6	
C2500 Sierra	L4	16	21	4.30/6	
G15/25 Rally	L4	14	16	4.30/6	
TOYOTA T100	L4	20	23	2.7/4	
Truck	A4	22	25	2.4/4	

Standard Pickup Trucks/4WD

CHEVROLET	Trans	City/Hwy		Eng/Cyl	Code
K1500 Pickup	L4	15	19	4.30/6	
K2500 Pickup	L4	14	18	4.30/6	
S10 Pickup	L4	17	21	4.30/6	
DODGE Dakota Pickup	L4	15	19	3.9/6	
Ram 1500 Pickup	L4	12	16	5.2/8	
Ram 2500 Pickup	L4	12	16	5.2/8	
FORD F150 Pickup	L4	15	19	4.9/6	
GMC K1500 Sierra	L4	15	19	4.30/6	
K2500 Sierra	L4	15	18	4.30/6	
Sonoma	L4	17	21	4.30/6	
ISUZU Pickup	M5	17	20	2.6/4	
NISSAN Truck	M5	18	20	2.4/4	
TOYOTA T100	L4	16	18	3.4/6	
Truck	L4	18	19	2.4/4	

Special Purpose Vehicles/2WD

CHEVROLET Blazer	L4	17	22	4.30/S6	P
C1500 Suburban	L4	13	17	5.70/8	
Lumina Minivan	L3	19	23	3.10/6	

	Trans	City/Hwy		Eng/Cyl	Code
CHRYSLER Town & Country	L4	17	23	3.8/6	
DODGE Caravan C/V	L3	21	25	2.5/4	
Caravan	L3	21	25	2.5/4	
FORD Windstar FWD Van	L4	17	24	3.8/6	
Windstar FWD Wagon	L4	17	24	3.8/6	
GEO Tracker Convertible	L3	23	24	1.6/4	
GMC C1500 Suburban	L4	13	17	5.70/8	
Jimmy	L4	17	22	4.30/6	P
HONDA Passport	M5	18	22	2.6/4	
ISUZU Rodeo	M5	18	22	2.6/4	
JEEP Cherokee	L3	17	19	2.5/4	
Grand Cherokee	L4	15	21	4.0/6	
KIA Sportage	M5	19	23	2.0/4	
MAZDA MPV	L4	18	24	2.6/4	
MERCURY Villager					
FWD Van	L4	17	23	3.0/6	
Villager FWD Wagon	L4	17	23	3.0/6	
NISSAN Pathfinder	L4	15	19	3.0/6	
Quest	L4	17	23	3.0/6	
OLDSMOBILE Silhouette	L3	19	23	3.10/6	
PLYMOUTH Voyager	L3	21	25	2.5/4	
PONTIAC Trans Sport	L3	19	23	3.10/6	
SUZUKI Sidekick 2-Door	L3	23	24	1.6/4	
Sidekick 4-Door	L4	22	26	1.6/4	
TOYOTA 4-Runner	L4	17	21	3.0/6	

Special Purpose Vehicles/4WD

	Trans	City/Hwy		Eng/Cyl	Code
CHEVROLET Blazer	L4	16	21	4.30/6	P
K1500 Suburban	L4	12	15	5.70/8	
K1500 Tahoe	L4	12	15	5.70/8	
CHRYSLER Town &					
Country	L4	16	22	3.8/6	

	TRANS	CITY/HWY		ENG/CYL	CODE
DODGE CARAVAN	L4	17	21	3.3/6	
FORD BRONCO	L4	14	19	5.0/8	
GEO TRACKER CONVERTIBLE	L3	23	24	1.6/4	
TRACKER VAN	L3	23	24	1.6/4	
GMC JIMMY	L4	16	21	4.30/6	P
K1500 SUBURBAN	L4	12	15	5.70/8	
K1500 YUKON	L4	12	15	5.70/8	
HONDA PASSPORT	L4	15	18	3.2/6	
ISUZU RODEO	L4	15	18	3.2/6	
TROOPER	L4	14	17	3.2/6	
JEEP CHEROKEE	L3	17	19	2.5/4	
GRAND CHEROKEE	L4	15	20	4.0/6	
WRANGLER	L3	17	18	2.5/4	
KIA SPORTAGE	M5	20	24	2.0/4	
MAZDA MPV 4X4	L4	15	19	3.0/6	
MITSUBISHI MONTERO	L4	15	18	3.0/6V6	
NISSAN PATHFINDER	L4	15	18	3.0/6	
PLYMOUTH VOYAGER	L4	17	21	3.3/6	
ROVER LAND ROVER					
DISCOVERY	L4	13	16	3.9/8	P
RANGE ROVER COUNTY					
LWB	L4	12	15	4.3/8	P
SUZUKI SAMURAI	M5	28	29	1.3/4	
SIDEKICK 2-DOOR	L3	23	24	1.6/4	
SIDEKICK 4-DOOR	L4	22	26	1.6/4	
TOYOTA 4-RUNNER	M5	19	21	2.4/4	

Special Purpose Vehicles/Cab Chassis

	TRANS	CITY/HWY		ENG/CYL	
BUICK COACHBUILDER					
WAGON	L4	17	25	5.70/8	
DODGE DAKOTA CAB					
CHASSIS 2WD	L4	15	19	3.9/6	

ANNUAL FUEL COSTS CHART

based on 15,000 miles per year

Est MPG	Dollars Per Gallon					
	1.90	1.70	1.50	1.30	1.10	1.05
50	570	510	450	390	330	315
49	582	520	459	398	337	321
48	594	531	469	406	344	328
47	606	543	479	415	351	335
46	620	554	489	424	359	342
45	633	567	500	433	367	350
44	648	580	511	443	375	358
43	663	593	523	453	384	366
42	679	607	536	464	393	375
41	695	622	549	476	402	384
40	713	638	563	488	413	394
39	731	654	577	500	423	404
38	750	671	592	513	434	414
37	770	689	608	527	446	426
36	792	708	625	542	458	438
35	814	729	643	557	471	450
34	838	750	662	574	485	463
33	864	773	682	591	500	477
32	891	797	703	609	516	492
31	919	823	726	629	532	508
30	950	850	750	650	550	525
29	983	879	776	672	569	543
28	1018	911	804	696	589	563
27	1056	944	833	722	611	583
26	1096	981	865	750	635	606
25	1140	1020	900	780	660	630
24	1188	1063	938	813	688	656
23	1239	1109	978	848	717	685

| | **Dollars Per Gallon** | | | | | |
Est MPG	1.90	1.70	1.50	1.30	1.10	1.05
22	1295	1159	1023	886	750	716
21	1357	1214	1071	929	786	750
20	1425	1275	1125	975	825	788
19	1500	1342	1184	1026	868	829
18	1583	1417	1250	1083	917	875
17	1676	1500	1324	1147	971	926
16	1781	1594	1406	1219	1031	984
15	1900	1700	1500	1300	1100	1050
14	2036	1821	1607	1393	1179	1125
13	2192	1962	1731	1500	1269	1212
12	2375	2125	1875	1625	1375	1313
11	2591	2318	2045	1773	1500	1432
10	2850	2550	2250	1950	1650	1575
9	3167	2833	2500	2167	1833	1750

Fuels of the Future

While everyone at one point or another hears how harmful gasoline is to the environment when it is burned in automobiles, very few have any knowledge of some promising alternative fuels that could replace or cut down the use of gasoline. The most current alternatives that have been developed to take the monster (gasoline) out of automobiles are methanol, ethanol, and natural gas.

Methanol

Methanol's claim to be environmentally sound stems from the fact that it is low in reactive hydrocarbons and toxic compounds. Compared to the diesel fuel that powers trucks and buses, methanol emits almost no particles and much less nitrogen oxide. The best thing about methanol is that it can be made from an assortment of carbon-based feedstocks, such as natural gas, coal, and such biomass materials as wood. Methanol is also much less flammable than gasoline and when it does ignite, the consequences are much less severe.

Methanol is, on the other hand, much more corrosive than gasoline, resulting in more damage to the fuel system, if not the car itself. This makes the fuel systems in methanol-powered vehicles much more expensive since stainless-steel fuel lines are needed. Methanol also doesn't have as high an energy-per-content ratio as gasoline but it does cost about half as much. You'll just need to have a much bigger tank to store it in.

Some cars have been built to handle a varying blend of gasoline and methanol. As a matter of fact, all of the major auto manufactures have produced a car that runs on "M85," a mixture of 85 percent methanol and 15 percent gasoline, with some success. Many experts believe that when methanol-fueled cars do gain in popularity they will have flexible-fuel engines, able to run on gas or methanol depending on the availability and affordability when it is time to fill up.

Ethanol
The beauty of ethanol is that it can be produced from corn, barley, rye, wheat, sugar cane, sugar beet, and many other crops. Ford and General Motors have already manufactured most of Brazil's fleet of ethanol-powered vehicles—which number over two million. Many service stations, especially in the midwest (since ethanol can be produced from corn), offer "gasohol," a mixture of 10 percent ethanol and 90 percent gasoline.

Natural Gas
Natural gas is one of the best alternatives for fueling trucks. Compressed Natural Gas (CNG) releases about 80 percent

fewer hydrocarbons, 90 percent less carbon dioxide, and 22 percent fewer nitrous oxides than does gasoline. It is also widely available from domestic sources.

The downside is that retrofitting a vehicle to run on natural gas costs around $2,000 a vehicle, and very few shops around the country are capable of making the switch. However, the installation price will eventually pay for itself since natural gas costs only about 75 cents for the energy equivalent of one gallon of gasoline. Another downside, of course, is finding a natural gas service station. Although natural gas is plentiful, there are only about 100 to 150 stations that carry natural gas, and once you fill up, it doesn't last long—only about as long as five gallons of gasoline.

Unfortunately, the greatest barrier to adopting these alternative fuels is uncertainty. Since no one knows what the next technology will be, few manufacturers are inclined to commit themselves to new fuels or build vehicles that depend on them. Consumers feel the same way; it's a risky move buying a vehicle that runs on fuel that's not widely available. To make matters worse, the huge oil companies have kept these fuels out of the mainstream. After all, they would have to produce and market these alternative fuels along with gasoline and diesel.

Electric Cars

Although electric cars have been around for a few years it is highly unlikely that you've seen one cruising around. The fact is, they just haven't caught on. It is amazing that car manufacturers haven't produced this virtually pollution-free vehicle to keep up with demand. Some manufacturers of electric vehicles have production back-up orders a few years long.

Why does a select group of individuals want electric cars? First of all, they are almost maintenance-free. They have no spark plugs, valves, mufflers, air or oil filters, hoses, fan belts, water or fuel pumps, pistons, radiators, condensers, points, starters, or catalytic converters—hence, no more tune-ups, oil changes, or radiator flushes, among other things. They are also much better for the environment than gasoline-powered cars; according to the California Air Resources Board, they emit 90 percent fewer pollutants than most gas cars, even less than the pollution generated from the power plant. They also don't need to be warmed up like normal cars, so they can start right up in any weather. Electric cars will also save you money on operating costs. The electricity needed to drive an electric car costs only about 3 cents a mile compared to about 6 to 8 cents a mile for a gas car that gets 25 MPG. This doesn't even include maintenance costs for a gas-powered vehicle.

If you find yourself wondering where to get one, hold your horses for just a minute. The electric car does have some drawbacks. First of all, they have the capacity to hold only about 50 to 75 miles worth of electricity before they need a four-to-eight hour recharge. This may not be bad if you have a ten-to-fifteen-mile commute every day—just plug it in at night and you're off. While these are huge drawbacks for the electric car, it won't be long until the problems are weeded out. It is up to the consumer to get the ball moving. If we demand them, they will be supplied.

5 The Office Supply Center

Using products that are harmonious with the environment is especially important in the office, where an abundance of products is used. When most employees arrive at their place of work, and observe waste, they get a message that management didn't mean to give. So the same environment-saving principles that you adhere to at home should be applied at the office. By using environmentally safe products at work and by following the tips in this chapter you can make conservation a motto to live by in the workplace.

Recycled Copy Paper

Considering how much copy paper is used in most offices, buying recycled copy paper is one of the best ways you can make a difference in your office. Hammermill is one company that manufactures recycled copy paper. A 500-sheet ream of 8½" by 11" paper lists for about $6.

Kenaf Paper

Kenaf paper is one of the newest alternatives offered to businesses and offices around the country. It is made from the fibrous kenaf plant and has tremendous environmental advantages over paper made from trees. One acre of kenaf produces 7–11 tons of usable fiber in a single growing season. An acre of forest on the other hand, requires 20–30 years to produce only 4–5 tons of useable fiber. After studying more than 500 plants, the U.S. Department of Agriculture chose kenaf as the most viable fiber plant for U.S. paper production. Since the paper is not as abundant as regular paper from trees, it is still a little more expensive. But buying products made from kenaf supports a much-needed market for alternative paper.

Recycled Notebooks

Buying recycled notebooks is another way to make a difference in the office. It saves trees and stimulates a much-needed demand for recycled paper products. Mead is one company that sells recycled notebooks. A 100-sheet spiral notebook of 100 percent recycled 8½" by 11" college-ruled paper costs about $1.89.

An estimated 45,000 trees could be saved each year if only 10 percent of the notebooks made in the United States were made from recycled paper. For every ton of paper recycled, seventeen trees, three cubic yards of landfill space, and 7,000 gallons of water are saved.

Recycled Folders

Manila file folders are now available from 100 percent recycled paper. They are just as durable as standard file folders but save trees.

Smead's recycled file folders contain at least 10 percent post-consumer waste. A box of 100, letter-size folders cost $11.75, and legal-size folders cost $15.25. Smead also makes hanging folders with at least 10 percent post-consumer waste. At 25 per box, letter-size folders cost $13, and legal size cost $16.

Esselte has file folders containing 10 percent post-consumer waste. A box of 100 costs $11.75 for letter size and $15.65 for legal size. Their hanging folders, with the same percentage of post-consumer waste, sell for $16.85 for a box of 25 letter-size folders, and $19.75 for a box of 25 legal-size folders. Sparco file folders, manufactured with 10 percent waste also, are sold in boxes of 100 for $11.60 for letter size, and $15.60 for legal size.

Shop around, because prices vary widely from store to store.

✿ Deforestation

Deforestation is perhaps today's biggest environmental threat. Worldwide, each year, over 35 million acres of tropical forest are permanently destroyed, an area the size of Florida. These fragile forests are home to over half of the earth's 5 to 30 million species, yet they comprise only 6 to 7 percent of its land surface.

What is causing all of this rain forest destruction?
• Approximately 25 percent of tropical rain forests are cut down due to commercial logging. As a result of new logging roads, formerly impenetrable forests are now open to peasant farmers and ranchers who further rape the land.

• These cattle ranchers and farmers are a major cause of deforestation. Thousands of acres are cleared each year for cattle pasture to produce beef for pet food and hamburgers on a worldwide scale. To make matters worse, cattle ranchers and farmers receive government tax incentives and support from foreign banks.

• Due to fragile and infertile tropical soils, many crop yields fail after only a few years, forcing the clearing of more forest for their short-lived cycle.

• Large scale development projects backed by major institutions such as the World Bank are being built in tropical rain forest countries. These projects, such as hydroelectric dams (that flood vast amounts of forests), colonization, and road-building projects, have wiped out tropical forests at an alarming rate.

What is the aftermath of all of this tropical forest destruction? For starters, it is a leading cause in global warming. These vast forests store carbon dioxide that people and animals spew out and turn it into living tissue—wood. In a single year, one healthy tree can absorb between 25 and 45 pounds of carbon dioxides. When the tree is burned down it not only releases carbon dioxides but also removes a part of nature that absorbs this greenhouse gas. As a point of interest, the burning of tropical forests produces about 20 percent of man-made carbon dioxide.

Deforestation is also wiping away thousands of species. Every day, at least one species of plant or animal becomes extinct as a result of deforestation! Their habitat is cut or burned and robbed of the resources for their survival. Animals aren't the only species that are wiped out. An estimated 140 million people call tropical forests their home. Their cultures are being destroyed due to the destruction of their natural resources and they are robbed of their land by cattle grazing and industrial activities. Though their lifestyles depend on the forests, many natives have existed without harming the ecosystem for generations.

Tropical forests also regulate the hydrological cycle of local areas by both absorbing and creating rainfall. Deforestation disrupts the cycle and causes extreme conditions such as flooding and drought. It is a cause of erosion and siltation in our rivers and oceans which can ruin drinking water and irrigation water. It also kills marine habitats and fish breeding areas.

Besides their aesthetic beauty and diversity, tropical rain forests provide us with an abundance of products that do not destroy the forests. These include a variety of food such as bananas, rice, eggs, coffee, peanuts, and chocolate. We also extract industrial products such as oils and latex used to make rubber. And more recently, we have found medicines and life-saving drugs such as curare, a paralyzing drug used in surgery; diosgenin, an active ingredient used in birth control; and many other medicines used to treat cancer, malaria, and heart disease.

Recycled Laser Printer Cartridges

Each year, about thirty million toner cartridges are sold, enough plastic waste to stretch almost halfway around the world. Next time you're in the market for a new toner cartridge, consider buying one that can be used over and over. They typically cost about half the price of a new one and save precious landfill space. Quill has a remarkable recycling service for laser cartridges. They are compatible with many Hewlett Packard, IBM, and Apple printers and are even upgraded in the refilling process so you get a higher quality. Simply send in your used cartridge and another remanufactured one will be mailed to you the same day you order (must be ordered by 6 p.m. your time). Call Quill at (708) 634-4800 for more information.

Use Compact Fluorescent Light Bulbs in the Office

Since lighting is one of the biggest energy users in most offices, replace your incandescent light bulbs with compact fluorescent bulbs. They are huge energy savers. (Refer to Chapter 2, The Hardware Store.)

Halogen Lighting

Halogen lights are another great way to save energy in your office, let alone landfill space. They work better than compact fluorescents for precise lighting, like for reading or working, and last much longer than incandescent lights. A typical 50-watt halogen light bulb costs about $4 and will last 2,400 hours—more than three times longer than a 50-watt incandescent.

Programmable Thermostats

A programmable thermostat lets you adjust the heating and cooling of your office at certain times. You can program it to turn down the heat or air conditioning in your office at night or during the weekend when nobody is there. They cost about $40 to $60 and will save you about 20 percent a year if used properly, and pay for themselves in less than a year.

Adhesives

Buy nontoxic tapes, glues, paper clips, staples, and string whenever possible.

Be sure to avoid glues that emit the smells of solvents, like hobby glue or rubber cement. Instead, use stick-type glue or basic white glue.

> ### ✒ Get an Energy Audit for Your Office
>
> Make sure your office gets an energy audit. Conducted by either the local power utility or a private energy consultant, it will prove to be a money-saving and environment-saving exercise. Energy audits are either free or very reasonable and should point out some very direct solutions to energy waste. A thorough office energy audit should include: 1) an assessment of current energy and water use, including how much electricity, heat, and water the office consumes and wastes; 2) an estimate of the actual costs of the energy consumed in the office; and 3) an estimate of the amount of energy wasted.

Here is a natural alternative to toxic commercial glue that you can easily make. It works great as paper glue. Mix 3 tablespoons of cornstarch with 4 tablespoons of cold water, and make a smooth paste. Then add the paste to 1½ cups boiling water and wait for the mixture to become clear. The mixture is ready to use when it cools.

Pens/Pencils

The environmental debate with writing utensils is whether to use a pen or pencil. There is no comparison if the pen is disposable and the pencil is made from cedar. The pencil can draw a line about thirty-five miles long while the ballpoint pen can draw a line only one or two miles long, so the pencils don't have to be replaced nearly as often. Furthermore, the pencil is made out of cedar, a renewable resource, while the pen is made of plastic, which comes from oil and doesn't degrade. Be sure to buy only pencils made from cedar and not to buy any pencils made in

Indonesia or that are unlabeled; chances are they are made from jelutong, a rainforest product that is logged at a dangerous rate. If you do use pens, as most of us do, avoid disposables.

Markers

Instead of using toxic solvent-based markers, buy china markers (wax pencils), colored pencils, or crayons.

Typewriter Correction Fluid

For correcting typewriter errors use tape that covers them up or lifts them off without the use of solvents. When fluid is a must, buy the water-based type made for photocopies instead of the solvent-based kind.

Scratch Pads

Eliminate the cost and waste of buying scratch pads. Simply use the other side of waste paper. A great way to collect it is to place a box next to your copier and persuade everyone to place bad copies with their clean side up in the container. Cut the waste paper in half, staple, and you have scratch paper pads. After using up the pads, simply unstaple them and recycle.

Packing Supplies

Recycle all packing supplies such as foam peanuts and padding. Instead of tossing them in the trash, reuse them to safely package all your shipping needs. Use a rubber stamp on the box to be shipped applying the message, "Please con-

❧ Creating a Green Office

Here are a few simple steps toward making your office earth-friendly:

—Be sure to recycle aluminum, glass, newspapers, and printer and copier ink cartridges. Office paper should also be separated and recycled. It will be astonishing how fast the pile of office paper will grow.

—Instead of relying on disposable foam or paper coffee cups and plastic eating utensils, encourage the use of ceramic mugs and metal utensils.

—Reduce your use of office paper. Be sure to print on both sides of the paper whenever possible. (Your paper expense will be cut in half.) Pass memos around rather than producing them for everybody.

—Buy recycled office paper, cards, letterheads, envelopes, etc. Educate the person in charge of ordering such items. Explain that supporting the recycling industry creates a demand for recycled goods and how important it is in the recycling process.

—Turn off equipment that is not in use. This is one of the biggest energy wasters in most offices.

—Instead of discarding broken office equipment, persuade the purchasing department to try to fix it first and to buy only durable products. If you must discard a piece of equipment or furniture, donate it to a local charity or to someone who will have a use for it.

tinue to reuse the packaging—help save the earth." If for some reason you don't have a collection of used packing materials, shred your waste computer paper and scrap paper to make your own.

Solvents and Detergents

If your office uses solvents and detergents such as paint thinners and cleaning supplies, dispose of them or other hazardous wastes at a collection site. Call your local environmental agency to determine how to recycle or dispose of leftovers. Or better yet, make your own cleaning supplies and materials; save the environment and money while you're at it. (See the cleaning section of Chapter 1.)

⚘ Pollution in the Office

Like mines and factories of the past, the office has become a highly toxic place to work. The following is a list of air and toxic pollutants that have had a detrimental effect on workers and the environment. If possible, avoid buying products with these toxins.

Asbestos—This may be the most dangerous and widely used toxin in the office. An estimated 50 percent of office buildings built between 1958 and 1970 used asbestos fibers for fireproofing and insulation. The bad news is, this cancer-causing air and water pollutant is released in the air as the buildings age and are repaired.

Benzene—This carcinogenic toxin causes skin irritation and can ruin the bone marrow's ability to produce red blood cells. It exists in photography supplies, spot removers, and an assortment of solvents and plastics.

Carbon Monoxide—This widely known gas is, of course, emitted largely by automobiles. Many offices, however, emit this colorless, odorless gas into buildings through their ventilation systems. It starves the body and brain of oxygen, causing headaches, dizziness, disorientation, and in extreme cases convulsions, coma, and even death.

Formaldehyde—This toxic chemical, also known as formalin, formal, and methyl aldehyde, is a recognized carcinogen, particularly of the nose and throat. Its symptoms are mucous membrane irritation, respiratory ailments, nausea, and dizziness. It is generally used as a resin in adhesives for making plywood and particle board. The toxin is discharged as building materials age.

Nitropyrenes—These crystals are found in Xerox brand and other photocopier toners. They are thought to be carcinogenic and mutagenic but have not yet been tested completely. Be sure to keep your copier in a well-ventilated area and wear rubber gloves and protective clothing when handling toners.

Trichloroethane—This solvent poses many health risks including liver cancer and many gastrointestinal, heart, and liver problems. It is an ingredient in processes ranging from cleaning machinery to decaffeinating coffee. It is present in many office supplies including typewriter correction fluid and typewriter and stencil cleaners.

Trinitrofluorenone (TNF)—This chemical is prevalent in photocopiers. It is not known whether it causes cancer yet, but the EPA and others suspect it does.

Company Cars

If you're in the market for a new fleet of company cars or trucks, be sure to buy the ones with the best gas mileage and service them at stations that recycle motor oil, tires, etc. Follow all of the tips and suggestions from Chapter 4.

Food

If your office or company has extra food from some occasion, say a catered event or company picnic, many shelter groups will take the extras as donations for the homeless.

"Environmentalize" the Bathrooms

Make sure all the bathrooms in the office building are energy and resource conservative. If possible install low-flow aerators automatic shutoffs on the faucets. Make dams in the toilets to conserve water and install electric hand dryers or cloth towels, instead of paper towels, to save trees.

6 The Appliance Store

This chapter covers the most energy-efficient appliances for your home. Appliances ranging from dishwashers to ovens and refrigerators to water heaters are included, along with "green tips" on using them, that should save you money in the long run.

Saving energy also saves our environment, since using less energy decreases the resources required to operate electric utility plants. Saving energy also decreases acid rain (since sulfur dioxide emissions of coal-fired power plants are one of the main contributors) and global warming (through the burning of fossil fuels such as coal, oil, and natural gas).

Comparing Appliances

Federal law requires that manufacturers disclose the energy efficiency ratings (EERs) or annual energy costs of seven major home appliances on yellow Energy Guide labels attached to the new appliances: boilers, clothes washers, dishwashers, heat pumps, refrigerators/freezers, room air conditioners, and water heaters. The ratings are derived from tests given by the manufacturers. These ratings are purely for energy efficiency and costs; therefore, they tell nothing about the appliances' extra features. For more information, pick up a copy of *Consumer Reports* magazine and/or yearly buying guide.

Refrigerators/Freezers

Just about every household in America has a refrigerator, one of the biggest energy users in most homes. A refrigerator consumes an average 1,000 kilowatt-hours of electricity each year. If your refrigerator was made before 1980 it might be a good idea to replace it. Refrigerators ten years old or older require about 30 percent more energy than today's models.

The problems arising from consuming energy aren't the only things refrigerators do to harm the environment. Most refrigerators cool with ozone-depleting CFCs (chlorofluorocarbons), also found in the foam insulation. By federal law, anyone disposing of a refrigerator must make sure that the CFC's in the cooling system are captured first. Your town may do the capturing when they pick up the appliance or you may have to pay a repair service to do the chore.

If you're in the market for a new refrigerator you should weigh your needs. Smaller machines, of course, use less energy. So if you live in a small household or eat out a lot, don't buy more than you need. Most important, don't cut corners when buying a new refrigerator. Although energy-efficient models may initially cost more, they last an estimated fifteen years. The accumulated energy savings will surely cover the difference in price and more than likely save you money in the long run. You will also be conserving natural resources. For more information, pick up a copy of *Consumer Reports* magazine and/or yearly buying guide.

🖉 Efficient Refrigeration

Although your refrigerator is one of your home's biggest
energy users, as mentioned earlier, there are many ways to
cut down on its energy use:
• Keep it full. This will cut down on the infusion of warm
air every time the door is opened.

• Plan well. If you're building a home or redesigning your
kitchen, plan ahead. Don't place your refrigerator right next
to the range or in direct sunlight—it will have to work overtime to stay cool.

• Clean your refrigerator coil at least once a year. Doing so
will keep your refrigerator from working overtime, and it can
make your refrigerator operate 10 percent more efficiently.

• If you're planning on leaving town for a week or more, save
energy by turning off the refrigerator and freezer (empty
them first, of course).

• Make sure your freezer is packed tightly. If the compartment is not full, add extra bags of ice to save energy.

• Your refrigerator should not be set below 38° F, your freezer below 5° F. Invest in a refrigerator thermometer to check
the settings. Setting it anything below these temperatures
wastes energy.

• Make sure there are no leaks in the door gasket. A good
way to do this is to turn off all lights in the kitchen at night
and place a bright flashlight inside. If you can see light coming through the seals the gasket is not a tight fit, hence,
energy is wasted. Another good test is to put a dollar bill in
the door and close it. If the dollar falls out you need a new
door seal or gasket. This test will not work, however, if you
have a magnetic seal door.

• If your refrigerator/freezer has a power-saver switch, make sure to use it. The switch controls the warming coils that prevent condensation on the outside in humid weather. Make sure it is in the off position during the winter and if you use air conditioning in the summer months it may be left off all year round.

• Be careful not to clutter the top of your refrigerator with too much junk. Bowls, bags of chips, and food containers can block the air-circulation path needed to keep the compressor working efficiently.

Dishwashers

Most of the energy used when running a dishwasher is for heating the water; therefore, an efficient water heater is a must. Contrary to popular belief, if you're like most people, using your dishwasher uses less water than doing your dishes by hand. (Believe it or not, on average, dishwashers use about 10 gallons of water compared to the 15 to 17 gallons it takes to wash and rinse the same load by hand.)

Dishwashers do, however, take different tolls on the environment. Since dishwashers aren't capable of scrubbing dishes as efficiently as a hand can do, they require harsher detergents to do an equivalent job. Dishwasher detergents pollute our water much more than regular dish soap. Dishwashers also use a tremendous amount of energy to heat the water and dry the dishes. And eventually, all dishwashers end up in a landfill.

What to Look for When Buying a New Dishwasher

The first thing to do when buying a new dishwasher is to figure out exactly what you need. If you live in a small household, a compact machine might do the job. Better yet, maybe you don't need a dishwasher at all. Since the energy used in running a dishwasher has the most impact on the environment, be sure to buy the most efficient one. Here are some key features to look for that will save energy.

- *booster water heater*
This device works by heating up your water heater's incoming water, thus saving energy by enabling you to set the water heater at a lower temperature.

- *multiple cycle wash*
This handy feature regulates the dishwasher for the size of the load. It conserves energy by using less water for small loads and more for large loads.

- *no-heat drying*

Although this feature means it will take a little longer for your loads to dry, it saves energy by letting your dishes dry naturally rather than having to heat up the air. It is the same concept as air drying your clothes, but not quite as time-consuming, and well worth the savings. For more information, pick up a copy of *Consumer Reports* magazine and/or yearly buying guide.

Kitchen Ranges

The big question when buying a new kitchen range is whether to buy gas or electric. Sometimes it isn't even a question; your house may lack the connection needed for a gas range. Half of Americans choose gas and half electric, but most choose free-standing. This, of course, doesn't help ease the decision, so let's go over their strengths and weaknesses.

Electric ranges are less expensive initially but much more expensive to operate. The biggest weakness for electric ranges is that they require electricity. They are only about one-third as efficient as gas ranges since they must convert electrical energy into heat energy. Gas ranges, on the other hand, simply pump natural gas directly from the ground into your range ready to burn. Environmentally, electric ranges don't even compare. Producing electricity takes a serious toll on the environment. It grossly contaminates our water, and pollutes our air so badly it comes back in the form of acid rain. Power plants spew out greenhouse gases and deplete our limited supply of fossil fuels while our wildlife's habitat is eradicated. Gas range burners turn on immediately and respond instantly, unlike electric burners, which take time to heat up and time to cool down and are visibly hot only at the highest setting. Electric burners on the other hand cook food faster than gas ranges. An electric coil burner heats 1½ gallons of water in about fifteen minutes. Gas burners take about ten minutes longer on average. Gas ranges are also known to have stronger baking capabilities than electric ranges but electric ranges are less expensive. And if you are going for the modern look, electric ranges look sleeker, especially the smoothtops.

When making a choice look over all the strengths and weaknesses for both ranges and match them to your needs. For example, if you have a house full of kids, a gas range might be a smarter choice for safety purposes. They cool down faster and are visible if hot, unlike electric ranges. And remember, electric ranges are much worse on the environment and your utility bills. For more information, pick up a copy of *Consumer Reports* magazine and/or yearly buying guide.

Washing Machines

Washing machines are one of the most popular appliances in American homes today. Seven out of ten homes are equipped with them and unfortunately most of them are top-loading models, which are much more energy intensive

✿ Efficient Cooking

(See page 19 for additional tips on conserving energy in the kitchen.)

—Make sure the gaskets in your oven door are not wearing away. The easiest way to do this is to try to slide a piece of paper through the gasket on the door and the metal on the (turned off) stove. If the paper can slide between the two or if you can see space then it is probably time to replace the gasket. Any heat loss in your oven will only result in energy loss.

—Check the vent filters on the back of your oven. Clean them if necessary and always keep the fan well lubricated to prevent energy loss.

—The burner flame of your gas range should always be a clean blue. Yellow flames indicate an adjustment that only your serviceman should do.

—Visually check the wiring components and burner of your electric range. If they look impaired they probably are and need to be substituted without delay.

—Be patient! Peeking in the oven when something is cooking is a tremendous waste of energy. Every time you open the door, heat is lost and the food takes longer to cook. Look through the oven door window whenever possible.

—Use lids whenever possible. This will not only reduce heat loss, but also speed up the cooking time.

—Try to match the size of the pot to the size of the burner so as not to waste any heat. For instance, put a six-inch pot on a six-inch burner instead of an eight-inch burner.

—Cook as many dishes at once as possible. Keep the oven at 350 ° F. If a recipe calls for a higher or lower temperature simply adjust the cooking time instead of the temperature.

> —Aluminum foil works great under the burners of electric ranges. It will keep food particles out of the mechanism while throwing the heat back up at your dish.
>
> —Only use your oven if the food you are cooking will not fit in your toaster oven. Why heat up extra space?
>
> —Always turn your electric burners or oven off a few minutes before your dish is done. The stored heat will continue to cook your food and you will save a small amount of energy.

compared to machines that load in the front. However, both have their pros and cons. Front-loaders use water and detergent much more efficiently than top loaders and take up less space. With a stackable dryer, both can fit in a closet or laundry room. Front-loaders also handle off-balance loads better than a top loader. Top-loaders on the other hand have a much larger capacity to handle family-sized loads, and they wash clothes faster than front-loading machines. You will also notice many more brands and models to choose from when shopping for a top-loading washing machine. For more information, pick up a copy of *Consumer Reports* magazine and/or yearly buying guide.

What to Look for When Buying a New Washing Machine

Fortunately, there are many features in washing machines that help out on their water, energy, and pollution levels. When shopping for a new one, make sure it is equipped with a switch regulating the size of the load. Doesn't it make sense for the machine to use only the energy it needs for that size load? Another nice feature to look for is a control that regulates the water temperature for different cycles. Why waste energy and use hot water during a rinse cycle?

> ## ✎ Efficient Washing
>
> —Always make sure your washer is full before running the machine. It takes much less water and energy to wash one big load than two small loads.
>
> —Since most of the energy consumed in a washing machine is for heating the water, try washing your load with cold water. Very rarely do you need hot water to clean your laundry.
>
> —If you insist on hot water for washing your clothes, at least rinse them in cold water. It does a better job and bypasses the need for energy to heat the water.
>
> —Be sure to place your new washer as close to your water heater as possible. The more pipe needed, the more energy loss. And wrap the pipes with insulation to maximize energy efficiency.
>
> —Never let your machine's filter get dirty. Follow the manufacturer's directions to keep it running efficiently.
>
> —Avoid using too much detergent. Too many suds make the machine work harder and, therefore, use more energy.

Some machines even have a button that will reuse wash water if you have a double water sink and a control that allows you to adjust the machine's speed. Turn it on super fast and shorten the time it takes to dry your clothes.

Clothes Dryers

Most American homes are equipped with clothes dryers. Virtually all new dryers will dry thoroughly and efficiently; there are, however, certain features to look for when buying a new dryer that increase its efficiency. The extras, of course, raise the price of the machine.

Gas dryers are definitely the way to go if you want to save energy. Since they are so efficient, they require about half the energy electric dryers do to dry the same load and take much less of a toll on the environment. Remember, generating electricity creates air and water pollution, acid rain, greenhouse gases, destruction of wildlife habitat, and fossil-fuel depletion. Natural gas, on the other hand, is pumped directly from the ground into your home, ready to burn and supply heat. Even though gas clothes dryers are more expensive off the bat, the savings in energy will pay the difference in as little as a year, then keep saving you money. Whether you choose a gas dryer is, however, contingent on whether you have the hookups or not.

Whether you choose gas or electric, be sure to buy a dryer with a control that senses the moisture level of the load. That way, the machine will turn off automatically when the clothes are dry, eliminating 10 to 15 percent wasted energy. Some machines have a temperature-sensing control. They work fundamentally the same way but turn

---

❧ Efficient Drying

—Since drying machines will keep running until everything is dry, separate weighty clothes (like jeans) from light clothes (like socks) for maximum efficiency.

—To keep your machine from working overtime, be sure to clean the lint filter after every drying and periodically check the vent for excess lint.

—If possible, install the machine in a warm part of your house to conserve energy.

—Check your dryer's outside vent to make sure it is not leaking cold air into your home.

the machine off when the temperature of the air reaches a certain level. They use anywhere from 5 to 10 percent less energy than regular dryers.

The most energy-efficient way to dry your clothes is to air dry them. This method, of course, uses 100 percent less energy than any clothes dryer. Drying racks and clotheslines are very inexpensive and do their intended job efficiently.

Air Conditioning

Though many people can't bear the heat of the summer without cooling themselves with air conditioning, it has many *un*cool environmental and economical costs that go with it. How many times have you gotten an electric bill during the summer and been amazed at how much energy it requires to keep cool (about 900 kilowatt hours a summer for the average room air conditioner). Now imagine that energy usage multiplied by fifty million, the number of central and room air conditioners pumping electricity from power plants each summer. (By now we should know the environmental damage of burning fossil fuels at power plants.) Even the most efficient air conditioners on the market use enormous amounts of energy.

The amount of energy required to operate air conditioners is only part of the problem. They supply cool air using a coolant which is a chlorofluorocarbon (CFC). A hydrogen atom is added that makes it possible for the molecule to degrade in the atmosphere. Although this added element isn't as harmful to the stratosphere as CFCs, it does deplete the ozone layer to some degree.

When making the decision of what type of air conditioning you want to cool your home, you must weigh your needs. If you need to cool only selected ares of your home, a room air conditioner could be your best bet. They don't cost as much as central air conditioners or split ductless air conditioners and are a breeze to connect, making them easy to move from room to room. Due to their size, they are not powerful enough to cool down an entire house. They work by taking heat from a room to the outside using a refrigerant like Freon or another type of harmful chlorofluorocarbon. Since heat is removed from the room, the room becomes cooler. When deciding which room air conditioner to buy, consider the cooling capacity (measured in BTU/hour), and the operating efficiency (measured by their energy efficiency rating, or EER).

If you would like to cool your entire home evenly, central air conditioning could be the call. Three out of every four new homes have it. It adds very little to the construction of a new home; however, if you are adding it to an existing home, it can be very expensive. The big expenses occur if you don't already have a forced-air heating system to run it through; you have to add ductwork. They have almost become a necessity in the South and parts of the Midwest to control humidity; however, they aren't effective at cooling selected rooms and are energy intensive to run, thus higher electric bills.

If your needs lie somewhere between room air conditioners and central air conditioners, you might want to consider a split ductless air conditioner. It represents a middle ground as far as price and capability. It is too expensive to use in place of a room air conditioner but might suit the needs of people who want to cool part of a house or for those who want to cool the entire house without the aggravation and expense of installing ductwork. Some are designed to work as a heat pump as well.

An EER (energy efficiency rating) sticker comes on all room air conditioners. Split ductless air conditioners receive a SEER (seasonal energy efficiency rating); they are, however, rarely displayed on units (ask the salesperson for ratings).

The EER of room air conditioners and SEER of split duct-less air conditioners can't be compared; they are determined differently. Central air conditioners are not listed because every house has different needs depending on installation and hardware. For more information, pick up a copy of *Consumer Reports* magazine and/or yearly buying guide.

Fans

The best alternative to air conditioners is fans. Fans can work up enough of a breeze to make you feel cooler but they can't take humidity out of the air. It is the same principle as the wind chill factor outdoors: the breeze can make a room that's 82° F feel like 75° F. Fans will also cut down your utility bills by reducing or eliminating your air conditioning needs. For example, an air conditioned room will feel much cooler with a breeze, enabling you to turn down the thermostat for the same effect. And fans use only a small fraction of the energy an air conditioner consumes.

Like all other appliances for your home, fans offer a variety of types to choose from. The most efficient are ceiling fans. For the small amount of power they need to operate, ceiling fans circulate more air than any other fan available. In spite of the fact that there is some minor wiring required for installation, the directions enable you to do it yourself.

Although ceiling fans are the most efficient, they are not as transportable as single room fans are. Portable fans are ideal for concentrating on a certain area since the wind can be directed anywhere.

Whole-house fans are still another option. Although they are the most expensive fanning system available and need to be installed by a professional, they are the most effective and efficient. They work by pulling air into your attic and substituting it with cooler air. Manufacturers claim that they eliminate the need for air conditioning altogether.

If a whole-house fan seems a little much for your needs, consider a window fan. They work by exchanging warm indoor air for cool fresh outdoor air. They are much smaller than whole-house fans but work great for certain rooms or areas of your house, and mount directly on the window. They also make them as box units perfect for transporting from room to room.

Garbage Disposers

Garbage disposers are a great way to help ease the problem of landfill space. They are the quickest way to move food waste out of your home and on the way to decomposition. Your excess food scraps gush directly from your sink to a sewage treatment plant or septic tank where they break down very rapidly. Landfills, on the other hand, can take years or even decades to break down food waste because oxygen has trouble reaching the scraps. Since dozens of municipalities realize the importance of garbage disposals in helping reduce dumping and incineration, they have mandated that all new kitchens come equipped with them. Not only are garbage disposers good for the environment, they also keep messy, odorous food waste out of your garbage cans.

Burning Wood for Heat

Many people in this country burn wood for heat. Unfortunately, most don't know the difference between various types of wood-burning appliances and waste a tremendous amount of wood. The following is a comparison among the types of wood-burning appliances. (A heater rated at 10 percent efficiency would require five cords of wood to produce the same amount of heat as one cord of wood burned in a stove rated at 50 percent efficiency, or by .63 of a cord by a stove rated at 80 percent efficiency.)

1. Traditional open masonry fireplaces—10 percent to 20 percent.
2. Masonry plus steel shell circulating fireplaces—10 percent to 20 percent.
3. Heat-storing fireplaces and masonry stoves—20 percent to 60 percent.
4. Franklin and other open-door stoves (run open)—30 percent to 45 percent.
5. Typical circulating stove—40 percent to 50 percent.
6. Noncatalytic high efficiency stoves—60 percent to 70 percent.
7. Catalytic stoves—65 percent to 75 percent.
8. "Dream Stoves" (theoretically possible)—more than 80 percent.
(Source: U.S. Department of Energy, Conservation and Renewable Energy Inquiry and Referral Service.)

Not All Woods Heat the Same
If heating your house with wood, look for woods that give off the most heat. Woods that give off the most heat are: black birch, hickory, live oak, locust, northern red oak, rock elm, sugar maple, and white oak. Woods that give off the least amount of heat are: alder, aspen, balsam fir, basswood, cedar, cottonwood, hemlock, northern white cedar, red fir, spruce, and sugar pine.

Commercial Fireplace Logs
Believe it or not, commercial fireplace logs are ideal for a quick evening fire. Although they cost much more than firewood, they burn for more than three hours and produce more than twice as much heat per pound as real firewood. They also burn much cleaner than real wood—80 percent

less carbon monoxide, 50 percent less smoke, 78 percent less creosote, 69 percent less particulate matter, and 50 percent less ash. Fireplace logs are also made of waste sawdust that would end up in landfills. And, even better, they are easy to get started!

7 Shopping for Baby

Baby products account for the largest consumption of disposable goods among all age groups. The truth is, disposable products are easy to use. This out-of-sight, out-of-mind mentality for baby products must come to a halt. The products are simply ruining our environment. We also need to change the toys we give our kids. Nature is too precious to buy the disposable toys of yesteryear, which only teach kids to consume more. After all, kids have to learn to love nature in order to protect it. So teach your children while they're young to love and protect the environment. You don't want them to blame you for the harm we pass on to their generation! Although there are not yet very many green products for the young, this chapters includes dozens of baby products that don't trash our earth, along with toys and gifts that will teach your kid to value nature.

Cloth Diapers

Use cloth diapers instead of disposables. The 18 billion disposable diapers Americans discard each year could stretch to the moon and back seven times! They take up to 500 years to decompose in a landfill and add an estimated 2.8 million tons of feces and urine to our overcrowded landfills, spreading harmful bacteria. Although an estimated 85 percent of American diaper users use disposables exclusively, cotton diapers can be used up to 100 times and take only one to six months to decompose. They can also be less expensive than disposables if used properly. Some experts estimate that diaper services can be half as expensive as disposable diapers, and they work just as effectively for your baby.

Over a billion trees are destroyed each year just to make disposable diapers. *Use cloth diapers!*

Baby Foods

Although most parents assume baby foods are a healthy and nurturing food, a growing number of parents are now questioning the purity of the ingredients, and they have been discovering many surprises. Many of the ingredients such as apples, carrots, and potatoes have been found to have a high level of residue from pesticides, and many baby-food companies have been caught putting synthetic ingredients in products being sold as 100 percent natural.

Fortunately there are alternatives to synthetic baby foods. The organic baby-food industry has caught on in the last few years. This awareness is a result of a 1989 study conducted by the Natural Resources Defense Council that warned parents of the lifetime risks of cancer for children stemming from pesticide residue in foods.

By far the most economically, ecologically safe way to

feed your baby is through breast-feeding (until it is time to wean) or by making the food yourself. Breast milk is ideally suited to meet your baby's needs. The babies receive their mother's immunities to disease and tend to be in better health overall. If you decide to make your own baby food, a food mill will turn out to be a great investment. It allows you to puree foods right at the table for your baby to eat. It is simple and you will have the peace of mind that the food is free from unnecessary additives and packaging, and most important, is healthy and balanced.

If breast-feeding is not a possibility, purchase powdered infant formula for your baby. It is far cheaper than ready-to-serve formulas and usually comes in aluminum cans that are easily recycled.

Besides the question of purity, the packaging of most baby products is environmentally and economically unsound. Single-serving containers are notorious throughout the industry for excess packaging and waste. When choosing a baby food, look for the biggest size possible and buy foods packaged only in recyclable containers, such as aluminum cans and glass jars.

To find out more about how to prepare food at home for your baby, read *The Natural Baby Food Cookbook* (available for $7.95 from bookstores).

Earth-Friendly Manufacturers of Baby Products

Earth's Best Baby Food
(P.O. Box 887, Middlebury, VT 05753; (800) 442-4221)

Earth's Best is one of the few makers of organic baby food. These products can be found at natural food stores nationwide, and by mail order in large quantities. Earth's Best also makes a line of vegetarian baby dinners that provide 3 to 4 grams of protein per jar, 1 to 2 grams higher than most meat-based baby food dinners.

Ecosport
(28 S. James St., Hackensack, NJ 07606; (800) 486-4326)
As mentioned before, this company, founded by two environmentally concerned parents, created a sportswear line that uses only natural fibers and is manufactured without bleaches, dyes, and harmful chemicals. They make everything from T-shirts and sweatshirts to baby crib sheets and blankets.

Environmental Toys

You will not be able to purchase the following individual games or toys directly from the manufacturer. Look in your favorite local toy store to see if these or similar items are available.

Stuffed Animals, Puppets, etc.
Believe it or not, stuffed animals and puppets help form a child's appreciation of animals and nature. Although they appear lifeless, kids treasure them and treat them like royalty. Some of them can even talk when a string is pulled, giving them even more life. They will quickly become your kids' best friends.

Solar Construction Kit
Real Goods (966 Mazzoni St., Ukiah, CA 95482; (800) 762-7325) offers this fun and educational kit for children five years old and up. Children can construct a helicopter, windmill, airplane, or water wheel, each with a solar-powered moving part. The kit comes with an electric motor, a

small solar panel, and over 100 plastic pieces. Your child will discover the world of solar power and learn to reuse resources. The kit costs $22.

Paper-Making Kit
Real Goods also offers a paper-making kit that recycles your old newspapers, grocery bags, and egg cartons and turns them into note cards, scrap paper, and drawing paper. The kit includes all the supplies needed for kids ten and up to make their own paper. It's a great way to teach kids the benefits of recycling! The kit costs $25.

Save the Whales—The Game
Animal Town (P.O. Box 485, Healdsburg, CA 95448; (800) 445-8642) produces "Save the Whales," a game in which the players work together to "save" eight great whales, fighting against oil spills, radioactive waste, and other forces. The game costs $34.

All in This Together
Available from Sister's Choice (1450 6th Street, Berkeley, California 94710, (415) 524-5804) is a cassette to help children learn about the disappearing rain forests, pet overpopulation, endangered species, and urban forests through folk, rock, and jazz music.

The Whale Game
Wildlife Games, Inc. (P.O. Box 247, Ivy, Virginia 22945, (804) 972-7016) produces The Whale Game, a board game with an objective of building a whale family and guiding it home. "Whale facts" on the game cards make it educational. Cost is $19.

Greenhouse Game

Animal Town (see above) also offers the "Greenhouse Game," in which players inspect their house room by room looking for unsafe household conditions.

Root-Vue Farm

This kit offers everything that is needed to set up a garden laboratory. Your kids will plant vegetable seeds such as carrots, radishes, and onions and watch them root and grow through a clear container. It costs $19.99 and includes everything from seeds and soil to container and labels. It is made for ages four and up.

Solar Radio

Real Goods (see above) offers a solar AM/FM radio that is powered by the sun during the day. The radio has a crank arm attached to give it power at night. For every minute of cranking, ten minutes of your favorite music, news, or sports can be heard. In case of emergency, the radio has a battery compartment in the back for two AA batteries and an adapter opening for DC 3V charging. It costs only $39 and won't waste electricity or batteries. Jade Mountain ((800) 442-1972) sells a Walkman-like Solar Sports radio powered by silicon cells and equipped with a built-in nickel cadmium battery that can be recharged through an external jack. It sells for $29.

Ant Farms

An ant farm is a great way to introduce kids to nature. Let them watch these tiny engineers build tunnels and homes instead of watching tunnels and homes blow up on TV. Kits run about $8.00 and include everything you need to get started.

Bird Feeders/Bird Baths

Bird feeders and baths are perhaps the best way to bring a part of nature right to your home, up close. Opes Kids makes the Schoolhouse Birdfeeders for kids. The kit comes with a bird identification chart and costs $14.99.

Critter Carnival

Exploratory makes Critter Carnival, a self-enclosed magnifying unit designed to help kids study bugs. It is a great way to get kids in touch with nature and learn about the bugs they collect. The kit costs $9.99 and comes with bug facts, a net, and tweezers.

Home Planetarium

Super Science makes the Star Theatre, a home planetarium for kids eight years old and older. It is the perfect way to introduce kids to astronomy. The theatre displays stars, planets, constellations, and their names on your ceiling or wall. A 56-minute audio tape on the myths and legends of the sky are included in the kit, which costs $24.99.

Outdoor supplies

Jr. Camping offers gear to introduce kids to the outdoors. They sell a binocular/compass set to let kids age five and up learn basic skills. The set costs only $7.00. They also offer a kids' survival kit which includes a signal mirror, flashlight, compass, whistle, signal/safety cards, and carrying case. The kit was designed for children five and older and costs $7.99.

Games That Don't Require Products

Although all of the above games and toys require products, there are numerous games that don't require anything. They are a great way to teach kids that they can still have fun without consuming. The following is a short list of the all-time greatest games that don't require any products. You probably played them when you were a kid.

Tag	Duck-Duck-Goose
Hide-and-Seek	Leapfrog
Follow the Leader	Red Rover
Spud	Hopscotch

Of course, the best way to introduce kids to the environment is to expose them to the environment. Take them on a hike or go camping the next time you want to spend quality time with them.

ENVIRONMENTALLY ORIENTED BOOKS FOR KIDS

Earth Book for Kids: Activities to Help Heal the Environment, by Linda Schwartz (Learning Works, Inc. 1990).

SOS Planet Earth: Nature in Danger, by Mary O'Neill (Troll Associates 1991).

Kid Heroes on the Environment: Simple Things Real Kids Are Doing to Help Save the Environment, edited by Catherine Dee (The EarthWorks Group 1991).

50 Simple Things Kids Can Do To Save the Earth (The Earth-Works Group 1990).

My First Green Book, by Angela Wilkes (Alfred E. Knopf, Inc. 1991).

The Nature Book: Discovering, Exploring, Observing, Experimenting with Plants & Animals at Home & Outdoors, by Midas Dekkers. (Macmillan Publishing Company 1988).

Biology for Every Kid: 101 Easy Experiments That Really Work, by Janice Pratt VanCleave (John Wiley & Sons, Inc. 1990).

Endangered Animals. A Ranger Rick Book (The National Wildlife Federation 1989).

Cartons, Cans and Orange Peels: Where Does Your Garbage Go? by Joanne Foster (Clarion Books 1991).

Recycle: A Handbook for Kids, by Gail Gibbons. (Little, Brown and Company 1992).

8 The Drug Store

The most prevalent environmental problems with personal care products are the packaging that goes into them and the harmful substances the trash releases into our air, water, and soil. Manufacturing companies have made little progress in making earth-friendly products; instead, they focus their packaging on providing convenience for the user. How many times have you bought a pocket-size bottle of cologne, toothpaste, or shampoo? Cosmetic companies are the masters of trial-size containers, not of bulk packaging. Along with earth-friendly cosmetic products, this chapter lists companies that do and do not test on animals.

Contact Lenses

If at all possible, buy long lasting contact lenses. Believe it or not, throwaways do pose a threat to the environment. It isn't the miniscule lenses that are filling up our landfills, it's the packaging that each set comes in. These disposable lenses are extremely expensive. A pair of soft lenses that most people use for a year or two costs only about $50, which is only a fraction of what disposable lenses cost—about $60 for a three-month supply of twenty-four, or about $240 a year!

Razors

Americans throw away two billion disposable razors and blades each year. The plastic doesn't degrade in landfills and they consume high quantities of energy and toxic chemicals to manufacture. Incinerating them also creates toxic air pollution. Instead of shaving with disposables, try using long-lasting metal razors and blades. Another alternative is to buy an electric razor. The energy used is nothing compared to the environmental costs of disposable razors.

Room Fresheners

Room fresheners pose a great threat to the environment and to yourself. Most commercial air fresheners contain aerosols, ammonia, synthetic fragrances, and other toxic substances. Most of them work by coating your nasal passages and deadening nerves to diminish your sense of smell.

The good news is that there are many natural alternatives that work just as well without harming the environment and your health. Prevention is of course the best way to eliminate smells. Aerate your home more frequently and find the source of rotten smells to eliminate them. To freshen your home naturally, put in each room a bowl of potpourri, a mixture of dried flowers, or a basket of herbs and spices that you can make up yourself. Each of these can also be boiled to release more potent natural fragrances. House plants are also good air purifiers.

Tampons and Sanitary Napkins

Believe it or not, tampons pose a huge threat to our environment. Each year, thousands of plastic tampon applicators are washed up on our public beaches. They often kill birds and fish that choke on them, and they are not very pleasant to see on the beach. Always buy biodegradable tampons and napkins and, if possible, buy sanitary napkins and tampons made with recycled and unbleached fibers. Also look for products with the least amount of packaging; do you really need to buy tampons that are individually wrapped in plastic packages?

Companies that make earth-friendly tampons include Seventh Generation in Colchester, Vermont 05446. Their phone is (800) 456-1177. Their tampons are whitened with Hydrogen peroxide—not bleach. They use a process called bleached chemi-thermal mechanical pulping. It requires half as much pulp as other processes.

There are many environmentally sound alternatives to using disposable tampons and sanitary napkins. Sea sponges, for example, can be cut to size and used simply by sterilizing and boiling them. However, this must be done before they are used and between menstrual cycles. An other alternative is to buy menstrual cups, which are made of a soft rubber. Worn internally, they hold fluid well. Both work well and can be purchased at health food stores, but some women prefer to use reusable cloth menstrual pads. They are simply washed and used over and over again and are sized for the perfect fit. Many drug stores and health food stores carry them, but you can order them directly from New Cycle, (707) 829-3154; or Sisterly Works, R.R. No. 3, Box 107, Port Lavaca, TX 77979.

Deodorants and Antiperspirants

Just how do antiperspirants work anyway? Well, believe it or not, they are made from aluminum salts which contain harsh chemicals that cause your skin to swell slightly. The swelling actually causes the sweat pores to close, denying exit to any fluids that should naturally leave your body.

How good for your body is this? you might ask. Ironically, the answers are quite alarming. After all, how could a chemical that makes your body retain its sweat be good for you? Although it hasn't been examined thoroughly, it is widely believed that the aluminum base in these antiperspirants is linked to Alzheimer's disease. Deodorants and antiperspirants also contain many chemical ingredients derived from nonrenewable fossil fuels. This not only depletes what we have left of our remaining fossil fuels but also pollutes our water and air in the process.

When shopping for deodorants and antiperspirants, look for ones made with natural nontoxic ingredients by companies who don't conduct inhumane animal testing. Also, shop for the ones with the least amount of packaging. By all means, stay away from aerosols!

There are natural alternatives you can use at home—for instance, baking soda. You'd be surprised how much a pinch of baking soda will do to absorb wetness and deodorize your body. Another alternative is deodorant crystal. It looks like a rock made of cellophane but is 100 percent natural and works great. All you do is moisten and apply to control moisture and odor.

Shampoos and Conditioners

The biggest environmental dilemma regarding shampoos and conditioners is their packaging. Most products come in plastic bottles destined for the landfill after only one use.

The best thing to do to combat the packaging problems is to refill the bottle with nature shampoos and conditioners at a natural products store. Or, if that is not an option, buy the largest container possible and refill smaller bottles if necessary.

The ingredients in these commercial products also pollute our water supply. Many plants that treat wastewater are not equipped to control these harsh substances. The result: most of the ingredients end up downstream, endangering aquatic species by stealing their necessary oxygen and using it to begin the long decomposition process.

So, you may ask, can something that harms aquatic life be safe for humans? To determine that answer many companies first test these products on animals under very inhumane conditions. After all, how could the tests be humane if the products are unsafe to use on humans? After testing, the animals are sacrificed. Don't support companies that conduct animal testing!

Companies that make natural shampoo include:

ShiKai, which makes henna-based shampoo. Contact them at P.O. Box 2866, Santa Rosa, CA, 95405.

Sirena makes natural-based products with no animal fat, coloring or dye, perfume, or synthetic detergents, and Sirena doesn't conduct animal testing. Contact them at (800) 527-2368.

Aubrey Organics makes 100 percent natural skin and hair care. Contact them at (800) 347-5211.

Hair Colors and Dyes

Hair colors and dyes are about as unnatural to the environment as they are to your hair. Just about all commercial brands contain strong petrochemicals, most of which are toxic if inhaled or absorbed through the skin. The chemicals they contain (like most other synthetic substances) pollute wastewater with carbon-containing compounds and dissolved salt compounds that oftentimes end up in the earth's groundwater. Some hair dyes are comprised of potent solvents made from methyl chloroform, a chemical that depletes the ozone layer when released.

If you must dye your hair, stay away from commercial name brands. They usually contain the harshest ingredients and conduct inhumane animal tests. Check your local health food store or ask your beautician for some natural products available in your region.

Henna-based hair coloring is another option. Made from tropical plants in Africa and India, henna is one of the oldest methods used. Through natural means, it gives hair a variety of hints that last for several months. Henna-based hair coloring products have gained in popularity in the last few years and are available just about anywhere hair products are sold.

- Light Touch. This company makes several shades of 100 percent henna and can be ordered from Heart's Desire, 1307 Dwight Way, Berkeley, CA 94702.

- Rainbow Research. This company presents ten different colors of hair coloring, all made from henna, chamomile, and marigold flowers. They can be ordered from Rainbow Concepts, (404) 886-6320.

Hair Sprays, Gels, and Mousses

These "hair stiffeners" have a harsh effect on the environment. They are highly overpackaged in nonrecyclable plastic containers which are energy intensive and highly polluting to manufacture. Some are still packaged in aerosol spray cans! And their ingredients aren't much better. They rely on synthetic resins and other chemicals to hold your hair in a certain position. Most of them are derived from petro-chemicals which deplete our supply of nonrenewable fossil fuels and contribute to air, water, and soil pollution.

If you have a need for a hair spray, mousse, or gel, look for brands made from simple, natural ingredients instead of synthetic chemicals. Unlike major-brand manufacturers of hair sprays, mousses, and gels, most companies who make natural products don't have the need to conduct animal test-ing. And if possible, buy products in the largest size con-tainers or refillable bottles.

If you insist on using commercial products that contain chemicals to manage your hair, be careful not to get it in your eyes or on your skin and take precautions not to inhale any of it. Only use it in a well ventilated area, and by all means keep the chemicals away from children and fire.

Nail Polishes and Removers

Commercial-brand nail polishes, hardeners, and removers depend on harsh toxic chemicals to work. Their production and disposal depletes our supply of natural resources and pollutes our water, air, and soil. They are also dangerous to inhale and contain carcinogenic substances. And when it comes time to dispose of the tiny, wasteful glass bottles, recycling is out of the question since they are infested with chemical residues. Since they end up crushed in a landfill, the chemicals usually end up seeping into ground water. As with most other cosmetics with toxic ingredients, make sure the companies you support don't conduct animal testing.

Unfortunately, there aren't many natural non-toxic sub-stitutes with simpler ingredients to use on your nails. The best option available is to go "au naturel," that is, don't polish your nails. After all, they are the color and strength they are supposed to be.

Soaps

Cleanliness may be next to godliness, but it's not very nice what some soaps and their packaging are doing to our environment.

Since Americans go through at least 500,000 tons of bar soap and 128 million quarts of liquid hand soap every year, what we choose to wash our hands with is of extreme importance. Most soaps are sold in packaging that cannot be easily recycled. It often comes wrapped in beautiful but slick paper, and gift soaps are packed even more elaborately, perhaps in foil or plastic. Worse than bar soaps are the liquid soaps, packaged in overly elaborate bottles intended to be used only once.

Ingredients in many commercially manufactured soaps come from animals. Others come from nonrenewable sources such as petroleum, whose manufacturing requires much energy. After such a product is used, it leaves an earth-hostile residue in our water.

It is better to seek out less complex alternatives to the soap your family has probably been using. Best are soaps made from a few plant-based ingredients, for instance, palm, coconut, or peanut oil.

Lotions and Creams

The ingredients in commercial brand lotions and creams come primarily from products derived from petroleum. The packaging is also extremely wasteful—usually plastic one-time-use, nondegradable bottles. And since many of the ingredients can be dangerous, companies often test them first on animals.

Buy only lotions and cremes made from natural products. After all, wouldn't you rather rub a natural substance all over your skin than something derived from petroleum? Even the natural, cruelty-free brands contain some synthetic chemicals, although to a much lesser degree. When shopping for these products look for ones with the least amount of packaging (in recyclable containers if possible) and ones that do not contain animal by-products. Also steer clear of companies that conduct animal testing. They are usually the ones with the harshest ingredients if they have to test them on animals.

Toothpastes

Toothpastes pose a surprisingly high risk to the environment. As crazy as it sounds, most of the major commercial toothpastes are derived from petrochemicals. These, of course, are a nonrenewable resource and very damaging to the environment to produce. These toothpastes are harmful to your health and usually packaged in a plastic squeeze tube or a wasteful pump also made of nonrecyclable plastic.

Always buy toothpastes with natural ingredients. Why submit yourself or the environment to harmful substances when natural ones are available? And by all means, buy the biggest size possible and avoid pump bottles, a perfect example of excess packaging. Be aware, however: many natural brands don't contain fluoride, a major plaque-fighting ingredient.

Cosmetics

Like just about all other personal care products, cosmetics pose a grave threat to the environment. They are among the most wasteful products as far as packaging goes and their ingredients aren't much better. Most of the big commercial cosmetic companies load their products with ingredients made from petroleum and other toxic chemicals. Along with polluting the environment, these substances have been found by the FDA to be harmful to your health. Since the effects of many of the ingredients are not known, cosmetic companies are also among the worst offenders in testing their products on animals in an inhumane fashion.

There are, however, alternatives to supporting these companies. The most obvious of course, is not using cosmetics such as foundation, lipstick, and eye liner. Many people believe, in fact, that most women look much better *not* covering up their faces with synthetic materials. When shopping for cosmetics, buy only ones with natural ingredients and simple formulas rather than petroleum-derived chemicals. Also, shop for cosmetics with the least amount of packaging and make sure it's recyclable if possible. And make sure the companies you support don't conduct animal testing.

Perfumes and Fragrances

Major brand perfumes and fragrances pose terrible risks to the environment. First of all, like many other cosmetics, they are derived from petroleum-based products and coal-tar derivatives, both highly polluting to our air, water, and soil, and nonrenewable. These toxins supposedly illuminate the natural odors or are used as preservatives. Perfume and fragrance makers are also some of the biggest supporters of animal cruelty. Animals are usually trapped and killed for certain parts of their bodies used to enhance the scent of these products.

Take, for instance, castoreum, civet, and musk, all scents added to perfumes and fragrances. Where exactly do they come from? Well, if you were going to get castoreum on your own, you would have to kill a beaver and extract it from its sex glands. Civet would be a little harder. You would have to find a civet cat and take the substance from its anal pouch. For musk, you would have to kill a musk deer and extract a sac near its navel to get the substance. And since major companies use synthetic chemicals in their products, inhumane animal testing is standard.

Try using perfumes and fragrances with simple natural ingredients that don't require animal testing. They will usually contain plant-derived essences and other natural substances rather than synthetic substances and petrochemicals. If you must rely on synthetic fragrances (which are much less expensive), choose ones from companies that don't conduct animal testing. The ones that don't conduct inhumane animal testing are, not surprisingly, the ones that bypass the harshest chemical ingredients. Also look for perfumes and fragrances in the largest size glass containers possible. If you favor a spray, employ a refillable pump atomizer.

Aerosol Cans

There are dozens of reasons to avoid the use of aerosol cans. The manufacturing of them uses a massive amount of energy and creates pollution at every step. The fine mist that sprays their active ingredients is very hazardous to your health when inhaled and the propellant gas is often flammable and toxic under pressure. Furthermore, the mist creates smog and has been a major cause in ozone depletion. And when it comes time to throw the can away, even more problems arise. The cans are not recyclable, don't degrade in landfills, and are dangerous to incinerate.

Although millions of people still use these environmentally harmful aerosol cans, there *are* alternatives.

A company called Biomatik USA Corp. makes an air spray bottle that requires the user to pump the applicator before every use. The plastic bottle can be refilled with almost any liquid, including paints, hair spray, and deodorants. They can be bought in many health food stores or direct from the company by mail. Send $4.99 each, plus $3 shipping and handling, to Biomatik, P.O. Box 2119, Boulder, CO 80306; or call (800) 950-MIST for more information.

Another company, Excell Container, in Somerset, NJ, makes an environmentally sound aerosol product called the Atmos gas-free aerosol delivery system. It resembles a pump-spray bottle, but emits a constant mist when pressed. The bottle is also partially recyclable. Although the inner part is disposable, the outer container is recyclable in some areas. Chanel, Estee Lauder, and Sergeant's Pet Products all use this container in some of their products.

Products that *Do* Conduct Animal Testing

According to People for the Ethical Treatment of Animals, as of May 1995 the following companies conduct tests on animals. People for the Ethical Treatment of Animals (PETA) is a national nonprofit animal protection organization dedicated to establishing and defending the rights of all species. PETA works through public education, research and investigations, legislation, special events, direct action, and grassroots organizing. With more than a quarter of a million members, PETA operates under the simple principle that animals are not ours to eat, wear, or experiment on.

To become a member or donate, write PETA, P.O. Box 42516, Washington, DC 20015-0516.

The following companies manufacture products that <u>ARE</u> tested on animals. Those marked with an asterisk (*)

have declared an official moratorium on animal testing. Please encourage them to announce a permanent ban. Listed in parenthesis are either examples of products manufactured by that company or, if applicable, their parent company.

Alberto-Culver Co. (TRESemmé)
2525 Armitage Ave., Melrose Park, IL 60160 • 708-450-3000

Alcon Labs
6201 S. Freeway, Ft. Worth, TX 76134-2099 817-293-0450 • 800-451-3937

Allergan, Inc.
2525 Dupont Dr., P.O. Box 19534, Irvine, CA 92713 • 714-752-4500 • 800-347-4500

Andrew Jergens Co. (Jergens)
P.O. Box 145444, Cincinnati, OH 45250 • 513-421-1400

Arm & Hammer (Church & Dwight)
469 N. Harrison St., Princeton, NJ 08543 • 609-683-5900 • 800-524-1328

Aziza (Chesebrough-Ponds)
33 Benedict Place, Greenwich, CT 06830 • 203-661-2000 • 800-243-5804

Bausch & Lomb
P.O. Box 450, Rochester, NY 14692-0450 • 716-338-5386 • 800-344-8815

Bic Corporation
500 Bic Dr., Milford, CT 06460 • 203-783-2000

Block Drug Co., Inc.
257 Cornelison Ave., Jersey City, NJ 07302 • 201-434-3000 • 800-365-6500

Boyle-Midway (Reckitt & Colman)
Box 7, Station "U", 2 Wickman Rd., Toronto, Ontario M825M5 • 416-255-2300

*Breck (Dial Corporation)
1850 North Central, Phoenix, AZ 85004 • 602-207-7100 • 800-528-0849

Bristol-Myers Squibb Co.
345 Park Ave., New York, NY 10154 • 212-546-4000

Braun (Gillette Company)
66 Broadway, Lynfield, MA 01904 • 617-596-7300

Calvin Klein (Unilever)
Trump Tower, 725 Fifth Ave., New York, NY 10022 • 212-719-2600 • 800-745-9696

Carter-Wallace (Arrid, Lady's Choice)
1345 Ave. of the Americas, New York, NY 10105 • 212-339-5000

Chattem, Inc.
1715 W. 38th St., Chattanooga, TN 37409 • 615-821-457

Chesebrough-Ponds (Unilever)
33 Benedict Place, Greenwich, Ct 06830 • 203-661-2000 • 800-243-5804

Church & Dwight
469 N. Harrison St., Princeton, NJ 08543 • 609-683-5900 • 800-524-1328

Clarion (Procter & Gamble)
11050 York Rd., Hunt Valley, MD 21030-2098 • 410-576-1291 • 800-572-3232

Clairol Inc. (Bristol-Myers Squibb)
345 Park Ave., New York, NY 10154 • 212-546-5000 • 800-223-5800

Clorox
1221 Broadway, Oakland, CA 94612 • 510-271-7000 • 800-227-1860

Colgate-Palmolive Co.
300 Park Ave., New York, NY 10022 • 212-310-2000 • 800-221-4607

Commerce Drug Co. (Del Labs)
565 Broad Hollow Rd. Farmingdale, NY 11735 • 516-293-7070 • 800-645-9888

Consumer Value Stores
One CVS Dr., Woonsocket, RI 02895 • 401-765-1500

Coty (Benckiser)
237 Park Ave., New York, NY 10017-3142 • 212-850-2300

Cover Girl (Procter & Gamble)
Box 1799, Baltimore, MD 21203 • 410-576-1291 • 800-543-1745

Dana Perfumes
635 Madison Ave., New York, NY 10022-1009 • 212-751-3700

Del Laboratories
565 Broad Hollow Rd., Farmingdale, NY 11735 • 516-293-7070 • 800-645-9888

*Dial Corporation
1850 North Central, Phoenix, AZ 85004 • 602-207-7100 • 800-528-0849

DowBrands
5601 E. River Rd., Fridley, MN 55432 • 612-571-1234

Drackett Products Co. (S.C. Johnson & Son)
1525 Howe St., Racine, WI 53403 • 414-631-2000 • 800-558-5252

EcoLab
Ecolab Center, St. Paul, MN 55102 • 612-293-2233 • 800-352-5326

Eli Lilly & Co.
Lilly Corporate Center, Indianapolis, IN 46285 • 317-276-2000

El Sanofi Inc.
90 Park Ave., 24th Floor, New York, NY 10016 • 212-907-2000

Elizabeth Arden (Unilever)
1345 Avenue of the Americas, New York, NY 10105 • 212-261-1000 • 800-745-9696

Erno Laszlo
200 First Stamford Pl., Stamford, CT 06902-6759 • 203-363-5461

Fabergé (Chesebrough-Ponds)
33 Benedict Place, Greenwich, CT 06830 • 203-661-2000 • 800-243-5804

*Faultless Starch Bon Ami Co.
1025 West 8th St., Kansas City, MO 61010-1207 • 816-842-1230

Fendi (Elizabeth Arden)
1345 Avenue of the Americas, New York, NY 10105 • 212-261-1000 • 800-745-9696

Flame Glow (Del Labs)
565 Broad Hollow Rd., Farmingdale, NY 11735 • 516-293-7070 • 800-645-9888

Gillette Co. (Liquid Paper, Flair)
Prudential Tower Building, Boston, MA 02199 • 617-421-7000 • 800-872-7202

Givaudan-Roure
1775 Windsor Rd., Teaneck, NJ 07666 • 201-833-2300

Helene Curtis Industries (Finesse)
325 N. Wells St., Chicago, IL 60610-4713 • 312-661-0222

ISO
Suite 1400, Merchandise Mart Plaza, Chicago, IL 60654 • 800-476-4247

Jhirmack (Playtex)
215 College Rd., P.O. Box 728, Paramus, NJ 07653 • 201-295-8000 • 800-222-0453

Johnson & Johnson
1 Johnson & Johnson Plaza, New Brunswick, NJ 08933 • 908-524-0400

S. C. Johnson & Son
1525 Howe St., Racine, WI 53403 • 414-631-2000 • 800-558-5252

Johnson Products Co.
8522 S. Lafayette Ave., Chicago, IL 60620 • 312-483-4100

Jovan (Quintessence)
980 N. Michigan Ave., Chicago, IL 60611 • 312-951-7000

Kimberly-Clark Corp. (Kleenex)
P.O. Box 2020, Neenah, WI 54957-2020 • 414-721-2000 • 800-544-1847

Lever Brothers (Unilever)
390 Park Ave., New York, NY 10022 • 212-688-6000 • 800-745-9696

L & F Products
One Philips Pkwy., Montvale, NJ 07645-1810 • 201-573-5700

*Mary Kay Cosmetics
8787 Stemmons Freeway, Dallas, TX 75247 • 214-630-8787 • 800-201-1362

Matrix Essentials, Inc. (Bristol-Myers Squibb Co.)
30601 Carter St., Solon, OH 44139 • 216-248-3700

Max Factor (Procter & Gamble)
11050 York Rd., Hunt Valley, MD 21030-2098 • 410-576-1291 • 800-526-8787

Maybelline
3030 Jackson Ave., Memphis, TN 38112-2018 • 901-324-0310

Mead
Courthouse Plaza, NE, Dayton, OH 45463 • 513-495-6323

Mennen Co.
Hanover Ave., Morristown, NJ 07962 • 201-631-9000

Naturelle (Helene Curtis)
325 N. Wells St., Chicago, IL 60610-4713 • 312-661-0222

Neoteric Cos. (Alpha Hydrox)
4880 Havana St., Denver, CO 80239-0019 • 303-373-4860

Neutrogena Corporation (Johnson & Johnson)
5760 West 96th St., Los Angeles, Ca 90045 • 310-642-1150

Neutron Industries, Inc.
7107 N. Black Canyon Hwy., Phoenix, AZ 85021 • 602-864-0090

Noxell (Procter & Gamble)
11050 York Rd., Hunt Valley, MD 21030-2098 • 410-785-7300 • 800-572-3232

Oral-B (Gillette Company)
1 Lagoon Dr., Redwood City, CA 94065-1561 • 415-598-5000

Pantene (Procter & Gamble)
10 Westport Rd., Wilton, CT 06897 • 800-543-7270

Parfums Int'l (White Shoulders)
1345 Ave. of the Americas, New York, NY 10105 • 212-261-1000

Parker Pens (Gillette Company)
P.O. Box 5100, Janesville, WI 53547-5100 • 608-755-7000

Pennex
1 Pennex Dr., Verona, PA 15147 • 412-828-2900 • 800-245-6110

Perrigo
117 Water St., Allegan, MI 49010 • 616-673-8451 • 800-253-3606

Pfizer
235 E. 42nd St., New York, NY 10017 • 212-573-2323

Physicians Formula Cosmetics
230 S. 9th Ave., City of Industry, CA 91749 • 818-968-3855

Playtex Corporation
215 College Rd., P.O. Box 728, Paramus, NJ 07653 • 201-295-8000

Prince Matchabelli (Chesebrough-Ponds)
33 Benedict Place, Greenwich, CT 06830 • 203-661-2000 • 800-243-5804

Procter & Gamble Co. (Crest, Tide)
P.O. Box 599, Cincinnati, OH 45201 • 513-983-1100 • 800-543-1745

*Purex Corporation (Dial Corporation)
1850 North Central, Phoenix, AZ 85004 • 602-207-7100 • 800-528-0849

Quintessence
980 N. Michigan Ave., Chicago, IL 60611 • 312-951-7000

Reckitt & Colman
1655 Valley Rd., Wayne, NJ 07474-0945 • 201-633-6700 • 800-232-9665

*Redmond
18930 West 78th St., Chanhassen, MN 55317 • 612-934-4868

Richardson-Vicks (Procter & Gamble)
P.O. Box 599, Cincinnati, OH 45201 • 513-983-1100 • 800-543-1745

Sally Hansen (Del Labs)
565 Broad Hollow Rd., Farmingdale, NY 11735 • 516-293-7070 • 800-645-9888

Schering-Plough (Coppertone)
2000 Galloping Hill Rd., Kenilworth, NJ 07033 • 908-298-4000 • 800-842-4090

Schick (Warner-Lambert)
201 Tabor Rd., Morris Plains, NJ 07950 • 201-540-2000 • 800-323-5379

Scott Paper Co.
Scott Plaza, Philadelphia, PA 19113 • 215-522-5000 • 800-835-7268

Shiseido Co. Ltd.
900 Third Ave., New York, NY 10022-4795 • 212-752-2644 • 800-223-0424

SmithKline Beecham
100 Beecham Dr., Pittsburgh, PA 15230 • 412-928-1000 • 800-456-6670

Sterling Drug
90 Park Ave., New York, NY 10016 • 212-907-2000

Sunshine Makers (Simple Green)
P.O. Box 2708, Huntington Beach, CA 92649 • 714-840-1319 • 800-228-0709

Sun Star
600 Eagle Dr., Bensenville, IL 60106-1977 • 708-595-1660 • 800-821-5455

3M
Center Bldg., 220-2E-02, St. Paul, MN 55144-1000 • 612-733-1110 • 800-364-3577

Unilever
390 Park Ave., New York, NY 10022 • 212-888-1260 • 800-745-9696

Vidal Sassoon (Procter & Gamble)
P.O. Box 599, Cincinnati, OH 45201 • 800-543-7270

Warner-Lambert
201 Tabor Rd., Morris Plains, NJ 07950 • 201-540-2000 • 800-323-5379

Westwood Pharmaceuticals
100 Forest Ave., Buffalo, NY 14213 • 716-887-3400 • 800-333-0950
Whitehall Laboratories
685 Third Ave., New York, NY 10017-4076 • 212-878-5500 • 800-322-3129

Products that *Do Not* Test on Animals

According to People for the Ethical Treatment of Animals, the following companies *do not* conduct tests on animals.

Those companies marked with an asterisk (*) manufacture vegan products—made without animal ingredients, such as milk and egg by-products, slaughterhouse byproducts, sheep lanolin, honey, or beeswax. Companies without an asterisk may offer vegan products.

*ABBA Products Inc., 2010 Main St., #1000, Irvine, CA 92714
ABEnterprises, 145 Cortlandt St., Staten Island, NY 10302-2048
A'belir, Inc., 305 Kingston Ave., P.O. Box 1933, Daytona Beach, FL 32115
Abercrombie & Fitch, 4 Limited Pkway. E., Reynoldsburg, OH 43068
*Abracadabra, Inc., P.O. Box 1040, Guerneville, CA 95446
Adrien Arpel Inc., 720 Fifth Ave., New York, NY 10019
*Advantage Wonder Cleaner, 16615 S. Halsted St., Harvey, IL 60426
*AFM Enterprises, 350 W. Ash St., #700, San Diego, CA 92101
African Bio-Botanica Inc., 602 NW 9th Ave., Gainesville, FL 32601
*Ahimsa Natural Care, 877 Alness St., Suite 12, N. York, Ontario, Canada M3J 2X4
Alba Botanica Cosmetics, P.O. Box 12085, Santa Rosa CA 95406
Alexandra Avery Purely Natural Body Care, 4717 SE Belmont, Portland, OR 97215
Alexandra de Markoff, 625 Madison Ave., New York, NY 10022
*Alexia Alexander Corp., 24937 West Ave. Tibbits, Valencia, CA 91355
*Allens Naturally, P.O. Box 514, Dept. M, Farmington, MI 48332-0514
Almay Hypo-Allergenic, 625 Madison Ave., New York, NY 10022
*Aloe Gold (Green Mountain), 2755 Highway 55, St. Paul, MN 55121
Aloe Up, Inc., P.O. Box 2913, Harlingen, TX 78551
Aloe Vera of America Inc., 9660 Dilworth, Dallas, TX 75243

Aloegen Natural Cosmetics, 9200 Mason Ave., Chatsworth, CA 91311

Aloette Cosmetics, 1301 Wright's Lane, West Chester, PA 19380

Alvin Last, 19 Babcock Place, Yonkers, NY 10701-2714

Alyssa Ashley, Inc., 1135 Pleasant View Terrace W., P.O. Box 299, Ridgefield, NJ 07657

*Amazon Products, 275 N.E. 59th St., Miami, FL 33137

Amberwood, Rte 1, Box 206, Milner, GA 30257

*American Merfluan, 2501 Spring St., Redwood City, CA 94063-3021

*American Safety Razor, P.O. Box 500, Staunton, VA 24401

*America's Finest Products Corp., 1639 9th St., Santa Monica, CA 90404

Amitée Cosmetics Inc., 151 Kalmus Dr., Suite H3, Costa Mesa, CA 92626

Amoresse Labs, 4121 Buchanan St., Riverside, CA 92503

Amway, 7575 E. Fulton St., Ada, MI 49355-0001

*Ananda Country Products, 14618 Tyler Foote Rd., Nevada City, CA 95959

Ancient Formulas, Inc., P.O. Box 1313, Wichita, KS 67206

Animals Love Us, 1053 Ranier Ave., Pacifica CA 94044-3828

An-Tech, 201 N. Figueroa, Los Angeles, CA 90012

Aramis Inc., 767 Fifth Ave., New York, NY 10153

*Arbonne International Inc., 15 Argonaut St., Aliso Viejo, CA 92656

Arizona Natural Resources, 2525 E. Beardsley Rd., Phoenix, AZ 85027

*Aromaland Inc., Rt. 20, Box 29 AL, Santa Fe, NM 87501

Aroma Vera Co., 5901 Rodeo Rd., Los Angeles, CA 90016-4312

Atlantis Labs, 4505 W. Hacienda, Suite B, Las Vegas, NV 89118

Atta Lavi, 443 Oakhurst Drive S., #305, Beverly Hills, CA 90212

Aubrey Organics, 4419 N. Manhattan Ave., Tampa, FL 33614

*Aura Cacia, P.O. Box 399, 716 Main St., Weaverville, CA 96093

*Auroma International, P.O. Box 1008, Silver Lake, WI 53170

*Auromére Ayurvedic Imports, 1291 Weber St., Pomona, CA 91768

Autumn-Harp Inc., P.O. Box 267, Bristol, VT 05443

Avanza Corp., 11818 San Marino St., Rancho Cucamonga, CA 91730

Aveda, 4000 Pheasant Ridge Rd., Blaine, MN 55434

*Avigal Henna, 45-49 Davis St., Long Island City, NY 11101

Avon, 9 W. 57th St., New York, NY 10019

Ayagutaq, P.O. Box 176, Ben Lomond, CA 95005

*Ayurherbal Corp., P.O. Box 1008, Silver Lake, WI 53170

*Ayurveda Holistic Center, 92A Bayville Ave., Bayville, NY 11709

*Auys/Oshadhi, 15 Monarch Bay Plaza, Suite 346, Monarch Beach, CA 92629

*Baby Massage, P.O. Box 51867, Bowling Green, KY 42101

Baja Beach, 1603 Aviation Blvd., #14, Redondo Beach, CA 90278

Barbizon International Inc., 1900 Glades Rd., Suite 300, Boca Raton, FL 33421

Bare Escentuals, 600 Townsend St., Suite 329-E, San Francisco, CA 94103

*Basic Elements Hair Care System, Inc., 505 S. Beverly Drive, Suite 1292, Beverly Hills, CA 90212

Basically Natural, 109 E. G Street, Brunswick, MD 21716

Bath & Body Works, 97 W. Main St., New Albany, OH 43054

Bath Island, Inc., 469 Amsterdam Ave., New York, NY 10024

Baudelaire, Inc., Forest Road, Marlow, NH 0345

Beauti Control Cosmetics, 3311-400 Boyington, Carrollton, TX 75006

Beauty Naturally, P.O. Box 4905, 859 Cowan Road, Burlingame, CA 94010

*Beauty Without Cruelty, P.O. Box 750428, Petaluma, CA 94975-0425

Beehive Botanicals, Inc., Rt. 8, Box 8257, Hayward, WI 54843

Bella's Secret Garden, 1601 Emerson Ave., Channel Islands, CA 94975-0428

Belle Star, Inc., 23151 Alcalde, #C11, Laguna Hills, CA 92653

*Benetton Cosmetics Corp., 540 Madison Ave., 29th Floor, New York, NY 10022

Beverly Hills Cold Wax, P.O. Box 600476, San Diego, CA 92160

Beverly Hills Cosmetic Group, 289 S. Robertson Blvd., 461, Beverly Hills, CA 90211

Bill Blass (Revlon), 625 Madison Ave., New York, NY 10022

*BioFilm, Inc., 3121 Scott St., Vista, CA 92083

*Biogime, 1665 Townhurst, #100, Houston, TX 77043

*Bi-O-Kleen Inc., P.O. Box 82066, Portland, OR 97282-0066

Biokosma, 121 Field Crest Ave., Edison, NJ 08818

Bio Pac, RR 1, Box 407, Union, ME 04862

Bio-Tec Cosmetics Inc., 92 Sherwood Ave., Toronto, Ontario, Canada, M4P 2A7

Blackmores, 2-30 Towne Center Dr., North Brunswick, NJ 08902

Black Pearl Gardens, 220 Maple St., Franklin, OH 45005

Bo-Chem Co., Little Harbor, Marblehead, MA 01945

Body Glove Skin & Hair Care, 406 Amapola Ave., Suite 105, Torrance, CA 90501

*Body Love Natural Cosmetics, Inc., Box 7542, 303 Potrero St., #4 & #9, Santa Cruz, CA 95061

The Body Shop Inc., P.O. Box 1409, Wake Forest, NC 27588

*Body Suite, 1050 Broad St., San Luis Obispo, CA 93401

Body Time (formerly The Body Shop), 1341 7th St., Berkeley, CA 94710

Bodyography, 10250 Santa Monica Blvd., Suite 305, Los Angeles, CA 90067

Bonne Bell, 18579 Detroit Ave., Lakewood, OH 44107

Börlind of Germany, P.O. Box 130, New London, NJ 03257

Boswell R & D Inc., 3875 Telegraph Rd., Suite A-342, Ventura, CA 93003

Botan Corporation, 7760 Romaine St., W. Hollywood, CA 90046

*Botanics Skin Care, 3001 South State, #29, Ukiah, CA 95482

Botanicus Retail, 7610 T. Rickenbacker Dr., Gaithersburg, MD 20879

*Brocato International, 7650 Currell Blvd., Suite 240, Woodburg, MN 55125

Bronson Pharmaceuticals, 1945 Craig Road, St. Louis, MO 63146

*Brookside Soap Company, P.O. Box 55638, Seattle, WA 98155

California Tan, 1100 Glendon Ave., Suite 1250, Los Angeles, CA 90024

CamoCare Camomile Skin Care Products, 130 E. 93rd St., New York, NY 10128

Carina Supply Inc., 464 Granville St., Vancouver B.C. V6C 1V4

The Caring Catalogue, 7678 Sagewood Drive, Huntington Beach, CA 92648

Carlson Laboratories, 15 College Dr., Arlington Heights, IL 60004

Carma Laboratories, 5801 West Airways Ave., Franklin, WI 53132

Carter's Naturals, 3A Hamilton Business Park, Dover, NJ 07801

Caswell-Massey, 121 Field Crest Ave., Edison, NJ 08818

Chanel, Inc., 9 West 57th St., New York, NY 10019

Charles of the Ritz, 625 Madison Ave., New York, NY 10022

Chatoyant Pearl Cosmetics, P.O. Box 526, Townsend, WA 98368

Chempoint Products, P.O. Box 2597, Danbury, CT 06813-2597

Chica Bella, Inc., Interlink 580, P.O. Box 02-5635, Miami, FL 33152

*CHIP Distribution Co., 8321 Croydon Ave., Los Angeles, CA 90045

Christian Dior, 9 W. 57th St., New York, NY 10019

Christine Valmy Inc., 285 Change Bridge Rd., Pine Brook, NJ 07058

Chuckles Inc., 59 March Ave., Manchester, NH 03103

CiCi Cosmetics, 1631 S. La Cienega Blvd., Los Angeles, CA 90035

*Cinema Secrets Inc., 4400 Riverside Dr., Burbank, CA 91505

Citius USA, Inc., 120 Interstate N. Pkwy., E., Suite 106, Atlanta, GA 30339

Citré Shine, 151 Kalmus Dr., Suite H3, Costa Mesa, CA 92626

CLARINS of Paris, 135 E. 57th St., New York, NY 10022

*Clear Vue Products Inc., P.O. Box 567, 417 Canal St., Laurence, MA 01842

*Clearly Natural Products, Box 750024, Petaluma, CA 94975

Cleopatra's Secret, 130 W. 25th St., 10th Floor, New York, NY 10001

Clintele, 5207 N.W. 163rd St., Miami, FL 33014

Clinique Laboratories, 767 Fifth Ave., New York, NY 10153

Color & Herbal Co., 2652 Vista Del Oro, Newport Beach, CA 92662

Color Me Beautiful, 14000 Thunderbolt Place, Suite E, Chantilly, VA 22021

Color My Image, 5025B Backlick Rd., Annandale, VA 22003

Columbia Cosmetics Mfg., 1661 Timothy Dr., San Leandro, CA 94577

Come To Your Senses, 321 Cedar Ave. S., Minneapolis, MN 55454

Comfort Mfg. Co., 1056 W. Van Buren St., Chicago, IL 60607

Common Scents, 134 Main St., Port Jefferson, NY 11777

Compar, Inc., 70 East 55th St., New York, NY 10022

Compassion Matters, P.O. Box 3614, Jamestown, NY 14702-3614

Compassionate Concepts, P.O. Box 61336, Fort Myers, FL 33906-1336

The Compassionate Consumer, P.O. Box 27, Jericho, NY 11753

Compassionate Cosmetics, P.O. Box 3534, Glendale, CA 91201

Concept Now Cos., 10200 Pioneer Blvd., #100, Santa Fe Springs, CA 90670

Cosmyl Inc., 1 Cosmyl Place, Columbus, GA 31907

*Cot 'N Wash, Inc., 502 The Times Building, Ardmore, PA 19003

*Cotswold Perfumery, Bourton on the Water, Gloucestershire GL54 2BU, England

Country Comfort, 28537 Nuevo Valley Dr., Nuevo, CA 92567

*Country Save Corp., 3410 Smith Ave., Everett, WA 98201

Crabtree & Evelyn, Peake Brook Rd., Box 167, Woodstock, CT 06281

Crebel Int'l, 4401 Ponce DeLeon Blvd., Coral Gables, FL 33146

Creighton's Naturally, 11243-4 St. Johns Ind. Pkwy. S., Jacksonville, FL 32246

Crème de la Terre, 30 Cook Rd., Stamford, CT 06902

*Crown Royale Ltd., P.O. Box 5238, 99 Broad Street, Phillipsburg, NJ 08865

*CYA Products Inc., 211 Robbins Lane, Syosset, NY 11791

*Davidoff Fragrances, 745 Fifth Ave., 10th Floor, New York, NY 10151

*Decleor USA, Inc., 500 West Ave., Stamford, CT 06902

*Deodorant Stones of America, 9420 E. Doubletree Ranch Rd., Unit 101, Scottsdale, AZ 85258

DEP Corporation, 2101 Via Arado, Rancho Dominguez, CA 90220-6189

Derma-E, 9660 Cozycroft Ave., Chatsworth, CA 91311

Dermalogica Inc., 1001 Knox St., Torrance, CA 90502

Dermatologic Cosmetic Labs., 360 Sackett Point Rd., North Haven, CT 06473-3103

Desert Essence, 9510 Vassar Ave., Unit A, Chatsworth, CA 91311

Desert Naturels, 83-612 Avenue 45, Suite 5, Indio, CA 92201

DeSoto, Inc., 900 E. Washington St., P.O. Box 609, Joliet, IL 60434

Diamond Brands, Inc., 1550 S. Highway 100, Suite 340, Minneapolis, MN 55416

Dr. A.C. Daniels, Inc., 109 Worcester Rd., Webster, MA 01570

*Dr. Bronner's "All-One" Products, P.O. Box 28, Escondido, CA 92025

Dr. Hauschka Cosmetics USA Inc., 59C North St., Hatfield, MA 01038

E. Burnham Cos., 7117 N. Austin Ave., Niles, IL 60714

E.S. Laboratories, 19009 61st Ave. NE, Unit 1, Arlington, WA 98223

Earth Friendly Products, P.O. Box 607, Wood Dale, IL 60191

*Earthly Matters, 2719 Phillips Hwy., Jax, FL 32207

Earth Science, 23705 Via Del Rio, Yorba Linda, CA 92687-2717

*Earth Solutions, Inc., 427 Moreland Ave., #100, Atlanta, GA 30307

*Earth Wise, Inc., 4600 Sleepytime Drive, Boulder, CO 80301-3292

Eberhard Faber Co., 4 Century Drive, Parsippany, NJ 07054

Eco Design Company, 1365 Rufina Circle, Santa Fe, NM 87501

Eco 1 Corporation, 1550 Berkeley Rd., Highland Park, IL 60035

Ecover Products, Carpenter Rd., P.O. Box SS, Philmont, NY 12565

Edward & Sons Trading Co., P.O. Box 1326, Carpinteria, CA 93014

Elizabeth Grady Face First, 200 Boston Ave, Suite 3500, Medford, MA 02155

EM Enterprises, 41964 Wilcox Road, Hat Creek, CA 96040

Enfasi Hair Care, 2937 S. Alameda St., Los Angeles, CA 90058

Epilady International, Inc., 39 Cindy Lane, Ocean, NJ 07712-7249

*Espial Corp., 7045 S. Fulton St., #200, Englewood, CO 80112-3700

*Essential Aromatics, 205 N. Signal St., Ojai, CA 93023

*Essential Products of America, 5018 N. Hubert Ave., Tampa, FL 33614

Estée Lauder 767 Fifth Ave., New York, NY 10153

European Gold, 33 SE 11th St, Grand Rapids, MN 55744

Eva Jon Cosmetics, 1016 E. California St., Gainesville, TX 76240

Everybody Ltd., 1738 Pearl Street, Boulder, CO 80302

The Face Food Shoppe, 185 Bruce Hill Rd., Cumberland, ME 04021

Facets/Crystalline Cosmetics, 8436 N. 80th Pl., Scottsdale, AZ 85258

*Faith in Nature, Unit 5, Kay St., Bury, Lancashire, UK, BL9 6 BU

Farmavita USA, PO Box 5126, Manchester, NH 03109

Fernand Aubry, Paris, 14 rue Alexandre Parodi, 75010 Paris, France

Finelle Cosmetics, 137 Marston St., Lawrence, MA 01841-2297

Flex (Revlon), 625 Madison Ave., New York, NY 10022

Florida East Atlantic Pet Products, P.O. Box 8631, Coral Springs, FL 33075

Focus 21 International, 2755 Dos Aarons Way, Vista, CA 92803

Forest Essentials, 1718 22nd St., Santa Monica, CA 90404

Forever Living Products, P.O. Box 29041, Phoenix, AZ 85038

*Forever New International, 4791 N. Fourth Ave., Sioux Falls, SD 57104-0403

For Women Only Sun Care, 2755 Highway 55, St. Paul, MN 55721

*IV Trail Products, P.O. Box 1033, Sykesville, MD 21784

Fragrance Impressions Ltd., 116 Knowlton St., Bridgeport, CT 06608

*Frank T. Ross, 6550 Lawrence Ave., E., Scarborough, Ont., Canada, M1E 4R5

Freeda Vitamins, Inc., 36 East 41st St., New York, NY 10017

Freedman Cosmetic Corp., Box 4074, Beverly Hills, CA 90213 .

*Free Spirit Enterprises, 2064 Denis Ln., Santa Rosa, CA 95403

Frontier Cooperative Herbs, 3021 78th St., P.O. Box 299, Norway, IA 52318

Fruit of the Earth, P.O. Box 152044, Irving, TX 75015-2044

Garden Botanika, 8624 154th Ave., NE, Redmond, WA 98052

Geoff Thompson's Facial Masque, 16535 SE Alder Ct., Portland, OR 97233

Georgette Klinger, Inc., 501 Madison Ave., New York, NY 10022-5699

Giovanni Cosmetics, 5415 Tweedy Blvd., Southgate, CA 90280

*Golden Lotus, P.O. Box 51867, Bowling Green, KY 42101

Golden Pride/Rawleigh, 1501 Northpoint Pkwy., W. Palm Beach, FL 33407

Goldwell Cosmetics (USA), 9050 Junction Dr., Annapolis Junction, MD 20701

*Goodebodies USA, 1001 S. Bayshore Dr., Suite 2402, Miami, FL 33131

Grace Cosmetics (Pro-Ma), 477 Commerce Way, #113, Longwood, FL 32750

*Green Ban, P.O. Box 146, Norway, IA 52318

*Green Mountain, P.O. Box 51867, Bowling Green, KY 42102

Greentree Laboratories, Inc., P.O. Box 425, Tustin, CA 92681

*Greenway Products, P.O. Box 183, Port Townsend, WA 98368

Gryphon Development, 767 Fifth Ave., New York, NY 10153

Gucci Parfums, 15 Executive Blvd., Orange, CT 06477

Guerlain, Inc., 444 Madison Ave., New York, NY 10022

H2O Plus L.P., 676 N. Michigan Ave., Suite 3900, Chicago, IL 60611

*Hair and New Direction, 300 Country Club Road, Avon, CT 06001

Halston Borghese Inc., 767 Fifth Ave., 49th Fl., New York, NY 10153-0002

*Hargen Distributing, Inc., 3422 West Wiltshire Road, Suite 13, Phoenix, AZ 85034

*Harvey Universal, 1805 W. 208th St., Torrance, CA 90501

Head Shampoo/Pure & Basic Products, 20625 Belshaw Ave., Carson, CA 90746

*Healthy Times, 461 Vernon Way, El Cajon, CA 92020

Heart's Desire, 1307 Dwight Way, Berkeley, CA 94702

Helen Lee Skin Care & Cos., 205 E. 60th St., New York, NY 10022

Henri Bendel, 712 Fifth Ave., New York, NY 10019

Herbal Products & Development, Box 1084, Aptos, CA 95001

*The Herb Garden, P.O. Box 773-P, Pilot Mountain, NC 27041

*h.e.r.c., Inc., 3622 N. 34th Ave., Phoenix, AZ 85017

Heritage Store, P.O. Box 444, Virginia Beach, VA 23458

Hewitt Soap, 333 Linden Ave., Dayton, OH 45403

Hobé Laboratories, Inc., 201 S. McKemy, Chandler, AZ 85226

Homebody (Perfumeoils, Inc.), P.O. Box 2266, W. Brattleboro, VT 05303-2266

Home Health Products, P.O. Box 8425, Virginia Beach, VA 23450

*Home Service Products Co., P.O. Box 245, Pittstown, NJ 08867

House of Cheriss, 13475 Holiday Drive, Saratoga, CA 95070

Huish Detergents, Inc., 3540 W. 1987 South, Salt Lake City, UT 84104

Iced Creme Facial Masque, 1001 Bridgeway, Sausalito, CA 94965

Ida Glae (Nature's Colors Cosmetics), 424 La Verne Ave., Mill Valley, CA 94941

Il-Makiage, 107 E. 60th St., New York City, NY 10022

Image Laboratories, 2340 Eastman Ave., Oxnard, CA 93030

i natural cosmetics (cosmetic source), 355 Middlesex Ave., Wilmington, MA 01887

*International Rotex, Box 20697, Reno, NV 89515

International Vitamin Corp., 209 40th St., Irvington, NJ 07111

IQ Products Company, 16212 State Hwy. 249, Houston, TX 77086

J.R. Liggett Ltd., RR2, Box 911, Cornish, NH 03745

Jackie Brown Cosmetics, 2122 Anthony Dr., Tyler, TX 75701

Jacki's Magic Lotion, 258 A St., #7A, Ashland, OR 97520

James Austin Company, Box 827, 115 Downieville Rd., Mars, PA 16046-0827

Jason Natural Cosmetics, 8468 Warner Drive, Culver City, CA 90232

JC Garet, Inc., 2471 Coral St., Vista, CA 92083

Jean Naté, 625 Madison Ave., New York, NY 10022

Jeanne Rose Herbal Body Works, 219A Carl St., San Francisco, CA 94117

Jessica McClintock Inc., 1400 16th St., San Francisco, CA 94103-5181

Jheri Redding (Conair), 1 Cummings Point Rd., Stamford, CT 06904

*Jil Sander Fragrances, 745 Fifth Ave., New York, NY 10151

Joe Blasco Cosmetics, 7340 Greenbriar Pkwy., Orlando, FL 32819

John Amico Expressive Hair Care, 7327 W 90th St., Bridgeview, IL 60455

*John Paul Mitchell Systems, 26455 Golden Valley Rd., Santa Clarita, CA 91350

*JOICO International, P.O. Box 42308, Los Angeles, CA 90042-0308

Jolen Creme Bleach, 25 Walls Dr., P.O. Box 458, Fairfield, CT 06430

Jurlique Cosmetics, 1411 Dresden Drive, Atlanta, GA 30319

Kallima International, 1802 Tobin Trail, Garland, TX 75043

Katonah Scentral, 51 Katonah Ave., Katonah, NY 10536

K.B. Products, 20 N. Railroad Ave., San Mateo, CA 94401

Keep America Clean (ABKIT, Inc.), 130 E. 93rd St., New York, NY 10128

Kenic Pet Products, Inc., 109 S. Main St., Lawrenceburg, KY 40342

*Ken Lange No-Thio Perm. Waves, 7112 N. 15th Pl., Suite 1, Phoenix, AZ 85020

Kenra Laboratories, 6501 Julian Ave., Indianapolis, IN 46219

Kimberly Sayer, 125 West 81st, #2A, New York, NY 10024

Kiss My Face, P.O. Box 224, 144 Main St., Gardiner, NY 12525

Kleen Brite Laboratories, Box 20408, Rochester, NY 14602

KMS Research, 4712 Mountain Lakes Blvd., Redding, CA 96003

*KSA Jojoba, 19025 Parthenia St., #200, Northridge, CA 91324

LaCosta Products, 2875 Loker Ave. East, Carlsbad, CA 92008

*LaCrista, P.O. Box 240, Davisonville, MD 21035

*LaNatura, 425 N. Bedford Drive, Beverly Hills, CA 90210

Lancaster Group, 745 Fifth Ave., New York, NY 10151

(1) Lancome (Cosmair), 575 5th Ave., New York, NY 10017

*L'anza Research International, 935 West 8th Street, Azusa, CA 91702

La Prairie, Inc., 31 W. 52nd St., New York, NY 10019

(1) L'Oreal (Cosmair), 575 5th Ave., New York, NY 10017

*Levlad/Nature's Gate, 9200 Mason Ave., Chatsworth, CA 91311

*Liberty Natural Products, Inc., 9120 SE Stock St., Portland, OR 97215

*Life Tree Products, P.O. Box 1203, Sebastopol, CA 95472

Lightning Products, 10100 N. Executive Hills Blvd., Suite 105, Kansas City, MO 64153

Lily of Colorado, P.O. Box 12471, Denver, CO 80212

Lime-O-Sol Company (The Works), State Road 4, P.O. Box 395, Ashley, IN 46705

Lissée Cosmetics, 2937 S. Alameda St., Los Angeles, CA 90058

Little Red's World, 720 Greenwich St., #7K, New York, NY 10014

Liz Claiborne Cosmetics, Inc., 1 Claiborne Ave., North Bergen, NJ 07047

Logona USA, Inc., 554-E Riverside Dr., Asheville, NC 28801

*Lotus Light, P.O. Box 1008, Silver Lake, WI 53170

*Louise Bianco Skin Care, Inc., 13655 Chandler Blvd., Sherman Oaks, CA 91401

M.A.C. Cosmetics, 233 Carlton St., 2nd Floor, Toronto, Ontario M5A 2L2

Magick Botanicals, 3412-K West MacArthur Blvd., Santa Ana, CA 92704

The Magic of Aloe, 7300 N. Crescent Blvd., Pennsauken, NJ 08110

Mallory Pet Supplies, 118 Atrisco Pl., SW, Albuquerque, NM 87105

*Marcal Paper Mills, Inc., 1 Market St., Elmwood Park, NY 07407

Marche Image Corp., Box 1010, Bronxville, NY 10708

*Martin Von Myering, 422 Jay St., Pittsburgh, PA 15212

*Masada, P.O. Box 4767, North Hollywood, CA 91617-0767

Masatey de Paris, Inc., 25413 Rye Canyon Rd., Valencia, CA 91355

Mehron, Inc., 100 Red Schoolhouse Rd., Chestnut Ridge, NY 10977

Melaleuca, Inc., 3910 S. Yellowstone Hwy., Idaho Falls, ID 83402-6003

*Mere Cie, Inc., 1100 Soscol Rd., #3, Napa, CA 94558

Merle Norman Cos., 9130 Bellanca Ave., Los Angeles, CA 90069

Metrin, 21640 North 19th Ave., Suite C101, Phoenix, AZ 85027

*Mia Rose Products, 177-F Riverside Ave., Newport Beach, CA 92663

Michael's Health Products, 6820 Alamodowns Pkwy., San Antonio, TX 78238

Michel Constantini Cosmetics, 1215 Lexington Ave., New York, NY 10028

Michelle Lazar Cosmetics, Inc., 755 S. Lugo Ave., San Bernardino, CA 92408

*Micro Balanced Products, 25 Aladdin Ave., Dumont, NJ 07628

Mira Linder Spa in the City, 29935 Northwestern Highway, Southfield, MI 48034

Mode de Vie, 2701 Sol Y Luz Loop, Santa Fe, NM 87505

Montagne Jeunesse, The Business Village, Broomhill Rd., London, UK, SW18 4JQ

Monteil Paris, 745 Fifth Ave., New York, NY 10151

Mother's Little Miracle, 930 Indian Peak Rd., Rolling Hills Estates, CA 90274

Mountain Ocean, P.O. Box 951, Boulder, CO 80306

Mr. Christal's, 1100 Glendon Ave., Suite 1250, Los Angeles, CA 90024

N/R Laboratories, Inc., 900 E. Franklin St., Centerville, OH 45459

Nadina's Cremes, 3600 Clipper Mill, Suite 140, Baltimore, MD 21211

Nala Barry Labs, P.O. Box 151, Palm Desert, CA 92261

Narwhale of High Tor Ltd., 591 S. Mountain Rd., New City, NY 10956

*Natracare, 191 University Blvd., Suite 129, Denver, CO 80206

Naturado Cosmetics, 7110 E. Jackson St., Paramount, CA 90723

Natural Animal, P.O. Box 1177, St. Augustine, FL 32085

*Natural Bodycare, Inc., 511 Calle San Pablo, Camarillo, CA 93010

Natural Chemistry Inc., 244 Elm St., New Canaan, CT 06840

Natural Organics, 548 Broadhollow Road, Melville, NY 11747

*Natural Products Co., 7782 Newburg Rd., Newburg, PA 17240-9601

*Natural Research People, Inc., South Route, Box 12, Lavina, MT 49046

Natural (Surrey), 13110 Trails End Road, Leander, TX 78641

*Natural Therapeutics Centre, 2500 Side Cove, Austin, TX 78704

Natural Touch, P.O. Box 2894, Kirkland, WA 98083-2894

Natural Wonder, 625 Madison Ave., New York, NY 10022

Natural World, Inc., 88 Danbury Road, Wilton, CT 06897

*Naturally Free, The Herbal Alt., Rt. 2, Box 248C, Lexington, VA 24450

*Naturally Yours, Alex, P.O. Box 3398, Holiday, FL 34690-0398

*Nature Cosmetics, 11818 San Marino St., Rancho Cucamonga, CA 91730

*Nature de France, 100 Rose Ave., Hempstead, NY 11550

*Nature's Best (Natural Research People), South Rte., Box 12, Lavina, MT 59046

*Nature's Country Pet, 1765 Garnet Ave., Suite 12, San Diego, CA 92109

Nature's Elements Int'l, 115 River Rd., Edgewater, NJ 07020

Nature's Plus, 10 Daniel St., Farmingdale, NY 11735

Natus, 4550 W. 77th St., Suite 300, Edina, MN 55435

Nectarine, 1200 5th St., Berkeley, CA 94710

Nemesis, Inc., 4525 Hiawatha Ave., Minneapolis, MN 55406

*Neocare Labs, 3333 W. Pacific Coast Hwy., 4th Fl., Newport Beach, CA 92663

*New Age Products, 16200 N. Highway 101, Willits, CA 95490-9710

New Cycle Products, Inc., 104 Petaluma Ave., Sebastopol, CA 95472

*Neway, Little Harbor, Marblehead, MA 01945

Neways, Inc., 150 E. 400 N., Salem, UT 84653

*New Moon Extracts, Inc., 99 Main St., Brattleboro, VT 05301

Nexxus, Box 1274, Santa Barbara, CA 93116

NFC, Inc. (Nature Food Centres), 1 Natures Way, Wilmington, MA 01887

*Nirvana, P.O. Box 18413, Minneapolis, MN 55418

No Common Scents, King's Yard, 220 Xenia Ave., Yellow Springs, OH 45387

Nordstrom Cosmetics, P.O. Box 12338, 1321 2nd Ave., Seattle, WA 98111

*Norelco, High Ridge Park, P.O. Box 10166, Stamford, CT 06904

North Country Soap, 7888 Country Rd. #6, Maple Plain, MN 55359

N/R Laboratories, Inc., 900 E. Franklin St., Centerville, OH 45459

NuSkin International, 145 East Center, Provo, UT 84601

NutriBiotic, 865 Parallel Drive, Lakeport, CA 95453

*Nutri-Cell, Inc., 1038 N. Tustin, Suite 309, Orange, CA 92667-5958

Nutri-Metics International USA, Inc., 12723 E. 166th St., Cerritos, CA 90703

Nutrina Company, Inc., 1117 Foothill Blvd., La Canada, CA 91011

*Oasis Biocompatible, 1020 Veronica Springs Rd., Santa Barbara, CA 93105

The Ohio Hempery, Inc., 7002 S.R. 329, Guysville, OH 45735

*Oil of Orchid, P.O. Box 1040, Guerneville, CA 95446

Oliva Ltd., PO Box 4387, Reading, PA 19606

Only Natural Inc., 14 Buchanan Rd., Salem, MA 01970

OPI Products, 13056 Saticoy St., North Hollywood, CA 91605

*Orange-Mate, P.O. Box 883, Waldport, OR 97394

Organic Aid, 8439 White Oak Ave., #106, Cucamonga, CA 91730

Organic Moods (KMS Research), 4712 Mountain Lakes Blvd., Redding, CA 96003

Oriflame Corp., 76 Treble Cove Rd., N. Billerica, MA 01862

Origins Natural Resources, 767 Fifth Ave., New York, NY 10153

Orjene Natural Cosmetics, 5-43 48th Ave., Long Island City, NY 11101

Orlane, 555 Madison Ave., New York, NY 10022

Orly International, 9309 Deering Ave., Chatsworth, CA 91311

"Otto Basics-Beauty 2 Go!", P.O. Box 9023, Rancho Santa Fe, CA 92067

*****Oxyfresh U.S.A.**, East 12928 Indiana Ave., Spokane, WA 99220

*****Pacific Scents Inc.**, P.O. Box 8205, Calabasas, CA 91375-8205

Parfums Houbigant Paris, 1135 Pleasant View Terr. W, Ridgefield, NJ 07657

Parfums Joop!, 745 Fifth Ave., New York, NY 10151

*****Park-Rand Enterprises**, 12896 Bradley Ave., #F, Sylmar, CA 91342

Pathmark Stores, Inc., 301 Blair Rd., Woodbridge, NJ 07095

Patricia Allison Natural Beauty, 4470 Monahan Rd., La Mesa, CA 91941

*****Paul Mazzotta Inc.**, P.O. Box 96, Reading, PA 19607

*****Paul Penders USA**, 1340 Commerce St., Petaluma, CA 94954

The Peaceable Kingdom, 1902 W. 6th Street, Wilmington, DE 19805

Perfect Balance Cosmetics, Inc., 2 Ridgewood Rd., Malvern, PA 19355-9629

The Pet Connection, P.O. Box 391806, Mountain View, CA 94039

PetGuard, Inc., 165 Industrial Loop S., Unit 5, Orange Park, FL 32073

*****Pets 'N People**, 930 Indian Peak Rd., Suite 215, Rolling Hills Estates, CA 90274

Pharmagel Corporation, PO Box 50531, Santa Barbara, CA 93150

PlantEssence, P.O. Box 14743, Portland, OR 97214-0743

*****Planet, Inc.**, 26 Silkberry Street, Irvine, CA 902714

Potions & Lotions/Body & Soul, 10201 N. 21st Ave., #8, Phoenix, AZ 85021

Prescriptions Plus, 25028 Kearney Ave., Valencia, CA 91355

Prescriptives, 767 Fifth Ave., New York, NY 10153

Prestige Cosmetics, 1330 W. Newport Center Dr., Deerfield Beach, FL 33442

Prestige Fragrances, 625 Madison Ave., New York, NY 10022

The Principle Secret, 5950 La Place Ct., Suite 160, Carlsbad, CA 92008

*****Pro-Tan (Green Mountain)**, P.O. Box 51867, Bowling Green, KY 42101

Professional Choice Hair Care, 2937 S. Alameda St., Los Angeles, CA 90058

*****Professional Pet Products**, 1873 NW 97th Ave., Miami, FL 33172

Pro-Tec Pet Health, P.O. Box 23676, Pleasant Hill, CA 94523

P.S.I. Industries, 1619 Shenandoah Ave, Roanoke, VA 24017

*****Pulse Products**, 2021 Ocean Ave., #105, Santa Monica, CA 90405

*Pure Touch Therapeutic Body Care, P.O. Box 1281, Nevada City, CA 95959

*Quan Yin Essentials, P.O. Box 2092, Healdsburg, CA 95448

Queen Helene, 100 Rose Ave., Hempstead, NY 11550

Rachel Perry, 9111 Mason Ave., Chatsworth, CA 91311

Rainbow Concepts, Route 5, Box 569-H, Toccoa, GA 30577

Rainbow Research, 170 Wilbur Place, Bohemia, NY 11716

*Ranir/DCP Corporation, 4701 East Paris, Grand Rapids, MI 49512

*Real Animal Friends, 101 Albany Ave., Freeport, NY 11520

(1) Redken Laboratories (Cosmair), 575 5th Ave., New York, NY 10017

Reviva Labs, 705 Hopkins Rd., Haddonfield, NJ 08033

Revlon, 625 Madison Ave., New York, NY 10022

Royal Laboratories, 2849 Dundee Road, Suite 112, Northbrook, IL 60062

*Royal Labs Natural Cosmetics, P.O. Box 900, Waterbury, CT 06708

Rusk, Inc., 606 Westmount Drive, Los Angeles, CA 90069

Rx For Fleas, Inc., 6555 NW 9th Ave., Suite 412, Ft. Lauderdale, FL 33309

*Safetex Corporation, 16101 Continental Blvd., Colonial Heights, VA 23834

Safeway, Inc., 4th & Jackson St., Oakland, CA 94660

*Sagami, Inc., 825 North Cass Ave., Suite 101, Westmont, IL 60559

*San Francisco Soap Company, P.O. Box 750428, Petaluma, CA 94975-0428

*Santa Fe Fragrance Inc., P.O. Box 282, Santa Fe, NM 87504

Santa Fe Soap Company, 369 Montezuma, #167, Santa Fe, NM 87501

Schiff Products, Inc., 1911 S. 3850 W., Salt Lake City, UT 84104

Scruples Salon Products, 8231-214th St., West Lakeville, MN 55044

Sebastian International, 6109 DeSoto Ave., Woodland Hills, CA 91367

*SerVaas Laboratories, PO Box 7008, 1200 Waterway Blvd., Indianapolis, IN 46207

*The Shahin Soap Co., 427 Van Dyke Ave., Haledon, NJ 07538

Shaklee US, Shaklee Terraces, 444 Market St., San Francisco, CA 94111

Shené Cosmetics, 22761 Pacific Coast Hwy., Suite 264, Malibu, CA 90265

Shikai (Trans-India Products), P.O. Box 2866, Santa Rosa, CA 95405

Shirley Price Aromatherapy, 462 62nd St., Brooklyn, NY 11220

Shivani Ayurvedic Cosmetics, P.O. Box 377, Lancaster, MA 01523

*Sierra Dawn Products, P.O. Box 1203, Sebastopol, CA 95472

Simplers Botanical Co., Box 39, Forestville, CA 95436

Simple Wisdom, 775 S. Graham, Memphis, TN 38111

Sinclair & Valentine, 480 Airport Blvd., Watsonville, CA 95076

*Sirena Tropical Soap Co., P.O. Box 797217, Dallas, TX 75379

Smith & Vandiver, Inc., 480 Airport Blvd., Watsonville, CA 95076

SoapBerry Shop Company, 50 Galaxy Blvd., Unit 12, Rexdale, Ontario M9W 4Y5

Sojourner Farms Natural Pet Products, P.O. Box 8062, Ann Arbor, MI 48107

Solgar Vitamin Co., 410 Ocean Ave., Lynbrook, NY 11563

Sombra Cosmetics, 5600 G McLeod N.E., Albuquerque, NM 87109

Song of Life, Inc., 152 Fayette St., Buckhannon, WV 26201

SoRik International, 278 Taileyand Ave., Jacksonville, FL 32202

Soya System Inc., 1572 Page Industrial Drive, St. Louis, MO 63132

Spa Natural Beauty, 1201 16th Street, #212, Denver, CO 80202

*The Spanish Bath, P.O. Box 750428, Petaluma, CA 94975-0428

Spare the Animals, P.O. Box 233, Tivorton, RI 02878

*The Spirit of Saint Alban, 441 Little Elk Creek Rd., Elkton, MD 21921

Sport Lavit, Inc., 300 5th Ave. S., Suite 20, Naples, FL 33940

St. Ives Laboratories, 9201 Oakdale Ave., Chatsworth, CA 91311

*Stature Field Corp., 1143 Rockingham Drive, Suite 106, Richardson, TX 75080

Studio Magic, 1417-3 Del Prado Blvd., Suite 480, Cape Coral, FL 33990

Sukesha (Chuckles, Inc.), P.O. Box 5126, Manchester, NH 03108

*Sumeru, P.O. Box 2110, Freedom, CA 95019

*The Sun & Earth Company, 741 Fifth Ave., King of Prussia, PA 19406

*SunFeather Herbal Soap Co., HCR 84, Box 60A, Potsdam, NY 13676

Sunrise Lane Products, 780 Greenwich Street, Dept. PT, New York, NY 10014

*Sunshine Natural Products, Route 5P, Renick, WV 24966

*Sunshine Products Group, 2545-D Prairie Rd., Eugene, OR 97402

Super Nature, 4 Civil Place, Bloomfield, NJ 07003

Supreme Beauty Products Co., 820 S. Michigan, Chicago, IL 60605

Surrey Inc., 13110 Trails End Rd., Leander, TX 78641

Symmetry Plus Inc., 46 W. 85th St., #4A, New York, NY 10024

TaUT by Leonard Engelmann, 9428 Eton, #M, Chatsworth, CA 91311

TerraNova, 1200 5th St., Berkeley, CA 94710

*Terressentials, 3320 N. Third St., Arlington, VA 22201

Thursday Plantation Pty. Ltd., P.O. Box 5613, Montecito, CA 93150-5613

*Tisserand Aromatherapy, P.O. Box 750428, Petaluma, CA 94975-0428

Tom's of Maine, Lafayette Center, Box 710, Kennebunk, ME 04043

*****The Total Shaving Solution,** P.O. Box 832074, Richardson, TX 75083

Trader Joe's Company, P.O. Box 3270, 538 Mission St., S. Pasadena, CA 91030

Travel Mates America, 1760 Lakeview Rd., Cleveland, OH 44112

Tressa, Inc., P.O. Box 75320, Cincinnati, OH 45275

TRI Hair Care Products, 1850 Redondo Ave., Long Beach, CA 90804

Trophy Animal Health Care, 2796 Helen St., Pensacola, FL 32504

*****Tropical Botanicals, Inc.,** P.O. Box 1354, 15920 Via del Alba, Rancho Santa Fe, CA, 92067

*****Tropix Suncare Products,** 217 S. 7th St., Suite 104, Brainerd, MN 56401

*****Truly Moist (Desert Naturels),** 83-612 Avenue 45, Suite 5, Indio, CA 92201

Tyra Skin Care, 9019 Oso Ave., Suite A, Chatsworth, CA 91311

*****The Ultimate Life,** P.O. Box 31154, Santa Barbara, CA 93130

Ultima II, 625 Madison Ave., New York, NY 10022

*****Ultra Glow Cos.,** P.O. Box 1469, Station A, Vancouver, BC, Canada V6C 1P7

Unicure, 4437 Park Drive, Norcross, GA 30093

*****United Color of Benetton,** 540 Madison Ave., NY, NY 10022

*****U.S. Sales Service,** 1414 E. Libra Drive, Tempe, AZ 85283

V'tae Parfum & Body Care, 576 Searls Ave., Nevada City, CA 95959

Vapor Products, P.O. Box 568395, Orlando, FL 32856-8395

*****Vegelatum,** P.O. Box 51867, Bowling Green, KY 42101

Vermont Soapworks, Rt. 7, Brandon, VT 05733

*****Veterinarian's Best,** P.O. Box 4459, Santa Barbara, CA 93103

Victoria's Secret, 4 Limited Pkwy,. Reynoldsburg, OH 43068

Virginia Soap Ltd., Group 60 Box 20 RR#1, Anola Manitoba, Canada ROE 0A0

Wachters' Organic Sea Products, 360 Shaw Rd. S., San Francisco, CA 94080

Wala-Heilmittel, P.O. Box 407, Wyoming, RI 02898

*****Warm Earth Cosmetics,** 1155 Stanley Ave., Chico, CA 95928-6944

Weleda, P.O. Box 249, Congers, NY 10920

The Wella Corporation, 524 Grand Ave., Englewood, NJ 07631

Wellington Labs., 2488 Townsgate Rd., Unit C, Westlake Village, CA 91361

*****Whip-It Products, Inc.,** P.O. Box 30128, Pensacola, FL 32503

*****Winter White,** P.O. Box 51867, Bowling Green, KY 42101

Wirth International, 2000 National Ave., Hayward, CA 94545

WiseWays Herbals, 99 Harvey Rd., Worthington, MA 01098

Wind River Herbs, P.O. Box 3876, Jackson, WY 83001

Wysong, 1880 N. Eastman Rd., Midland, MI 48640

Yves Rocher, 1305 Goshen Pkwy., Westchester, PA 19380-2672

Zia Cosmetics, 410 Townsend St., 2nd Fl., San Francisco, CA 94107-1524

Zinzaré International, 11308 Hartland St., N. Hollywood, CA 91605

Zotos International, Inc., 100 Tokeneke Rd., Darien, CT 06820-1005

(1) L'Oreal has signed PETA's Statement of Assurance and has told PETA in face to face meetings that the company no longer conducts animal tests of any kind. However, later, when L'Oreal executives were asked to guarantee in writing that they will not test ingredients on animals, they refused.

The companies listed below offer a cruelty-free mail order business. Please contact them for catalogs and ordering information.

ABEnterprises, 145 Cortlandt St., Staten Island, NY 10302-2048

Amberwood, Route 1, Box 206, Milner, GA 30257

Animals Love Us!, 1053 Rainier Ave., Pacifica, CA 94044-3829

Ayagutaq, Box 176, Ben Lomond, CA 95005

Basically Natural, 109 E. G St., Brunswick, MD 21716

Bath Island, Inc., 469 Amsterdam Ave., New York, NY 10024

Baubiologie Hardware, 207-B 16th St., Pacific Grove, CA 93950

Baudelaire, Forest Rd., Marlow, NH 03456

Beauty Naturally, P.O. Box 4905, 859 Cowan Rd., Burlingame, CA 94010

*Body Suite, 1050 Broad St., San Luis Obispo, CA 93401

The Caring Catalog, 7678 Sagewood Dr., Huntington Beach, CA 92648

Common Scents, 134 Main St., Port Jefferson, NY 11777

Compassionate Concepts, P.O. Box 61336, Ft. Myers, FL 33906-1336

The Compassionate Consumer, Box 27, Jericho, NY 11753

Compassionate Cosmetics, Box 3534, Glendale, CA 91201

Compassion Matter, P.O. Box 3614, Jamestown, NY 14702-3614

EM Enterprises, 41964 Wilcox Rd., Hat Creek, CA 96040

Everybody, 1738 Pearl St., Boulder, CO 80302

Heart's Desire, 1307 Dwight Way, Berkeley, CA 94702

Little Red's World, 720 Greenwich St., #7K, New York, NY 10014

Lotus East InterNaturals, P.O. Box 1008, Silver Lake, WI 53170

The Peaceable Kingdom, 1902 W. 6th St., Wilmington, DE 19805

Rainbow Concepts, Route 5, Box 569-H, Toccoa, GA 30577

Spare the Animals, P.O. Box 233, Tiverton, RI 02878

Stepping Stones (formerly Blue Rhubarb), P.O. Box 6, Cambria, CA 93428

Steps in Health, Ltd., P.O. Box 1409, Lake Grove, NY 11755

Sunrise Lane Products, 780 Greenwich St., New York, NY 10014

Super Nature, 4 Civic Place, Bloomfield, NJ 07003

9 The Garden Center

Gardening is one of the best things you can do for the environment, if you do it correctly. According to the EPA, however, lawns and gardens receive the most pesticides of any land in the United States (about fifty million pounds a year). But if "chemical free" practices are employed, your lawn and garden can contribute positively to our environment. Your vegetation can absorb harmful carbon dioxide that would otherwise be released into the atmosphere and contribute to global warming. Even better, gardening reduces the cost of buying vegetables at the grocery store and alleviates the wasted energy and pollution that modern agriculture is known for.

This chapter informs you of many products and tips to make your garden contribute positively to our earth instead of harming it. It includes information on dozens of products ranging from fertilizers to lawn mowers. It also gives helpful information on products to avoid, and their alternatives.

Discontinue Pesticide Use

As you may already know, pesticide use is risky business. Out of the 600 principal ingredients in commercial pesticides only about 120 of them have been tested by the EPA for short- and long-term health effects. So for the most part, the pesticide you choose to use is a health and safety gamble.

We know that much of the pesticides used for nonagricultural purposes such as lawns and gardens are carried by the wind and groundwater, which means it pollutes our rivers, lakes, and streams. Furthermore, creatures like dogs, cats, and squirrels that dine on these chemical-laden edibles are also at great risk. And unfortunately, humans dine on these dangerous chemicals as well. Although only a few have been tested by the EPA (who have labeled many of them as "probably" or "possibly" carcinogenic), it is widely believed that many of the pesticides we ingest are highly toxic.

Pesticide-Free Commercial Products

Manure
Manure is one of the best natural fertilizers available. It contains plenty of nutrients and enhances the quality of the soil. Bovine, equine, or chicken manure—dried—works best and has the perfect nitrogen composition for most gardens. You can either haul it away yourself or buy it at your local garden supply store.

Commercial Natural Fertilizers
Commercial natural fertilizers consist of organic matter from seaweed, plants, fish, etc., all renewable resources. These fertilizers work well for root growth, use much less energy to manufacture, and create far less pollution than chemical fertilizers.

Mineral Fertilizers

Mineral fertilizers, available at agricultural suppliers and garden supply centers, add primary elements to your soils and balance its pH. The minerals are relatively easy to process and come from rich natural sediments.

Create Your Own Fertilizer with Compost

Rather than buying commercial products to fertilize your lawn and garden, turn your extra food waste and yard refuse into a rich fertilizer. The fertilizer will add much-needed nutrients and humus to your soil, improving its capacity to hold air and water. Composting is easy. All you have to do is build or buy a bin for your backyard to store your excess organic matter and stir it frequently to air it out and eliminate odors. You need four sturdy poles or wooden boards and some chicken wire. Drive the poles into the ground to form a square and wrap chicken wire around three sides of it. If possible, locate your pile in a cool damp shady spot or sprinkle water on the pile to quicken the decomposing process. In compost piles, billions of organisms break down the organic refuse into a form that can be used by plants.

Once the compost bin is built, you're ready to go. Keep a lidded plastic container in the kitchen to collect just about all food scraps except meat, cheeses, and grease. (They attract rodents.) When it's full, just stir it into the compost pile outdoors and soon you will have rich dark humus.

Some towns have their own composting programs in which all you have to do is bring your organic waste to a site and take home free compost. If your town doesn't yet have a composting program, encourage one. It costs at least $65 per ton to dump solid waste in a landfill and only around $35 per ton for municipal composting.

Composting not only helps your soil and your pocketbook but also decreases the amount of solid waste being dumped into our crowded landfills. If everyone in America did this we would save about 15 percent to 20 percent of precious landfill space every year.

Organic Pesticides

As mentioned above, commercial pesticides are destroying our environment. It doesn't have to be this way, though. There are many organic pesticides that you can probably find on the shelves of your kitchen. The following is a list of effective nontoxic pesticides that contain no harsh chemicals.

- Mix one teaspoon of liquid dishwashing detergent with one cup of vegetable oil. Shake it vigorously and add it to a quart of tap water. Use the solution as a contact insecticide, spraying the mix directly on the pests at ten-day intervals. It works well against white flies, spider mites, aphids, and various insects on carrots, celery, cucumbers, eggplants, peppers, and others. Before spraying all of your plants, test the solution on a single plant; sometimes it causes tip burn.

- Mix one teaspoon of liquid dishwashing detergent plus one cup of rubbing alcohol into one quart of water. Spray the mix on the tops and bottoms of leaves or dip small potted plants (inverted) into the solution every seven days or so. Make sure to test the solution on a few leaves at first to make sure no harm is done to sensitive plants.

- Soak three tablespoons of dry, crushed hot pepper in ½ cup hot water covered for a half hour. Strain out the particles of peppers, and then mix the solution with the liquid detergent formula mentioned above. This solution works well against a number of insects for both indoor and outdoor plants. Be sure to apply the solution to plants outside, though; the fumes can cause irritation to eyes and nose. Hot Tabasco sauce or Louisiana hot sauce can be substituted for hot pepper.

- Pyrethrin is another great natural insecticide. It is derived from the pyrethrum plant and is highly effective against a wide range of insects. It should be used according to the manufacturer's instructions.

- Lime sulfur is one of the oldest methods to get rid of pests. It is applied during the dormant period to kill most species of mites as well as mite eggs and those of many other insects. Lime sulfur can also be used on fruit trees and ornamentals due to its fungicidal value. Be careful not to use lime sulfur near your house, as it has been known to stain paint.

- Sabadilla is a great way to get rid of squash bugs and stink bugs. It is made from the seeds of a South American lily and can irritate eyes and lungs if not used according to the manufacturer's directions.

- Garlic and onions work great to get rid of aphids and apple borers. Grind up raw onions or garlic into a puree and soak in warm water overnight before straining. The liquid can be sprayed on roses, fruit trees, and flowers. Scrape any loose bark from the tree and swab liquid on it to be even more effective.

- Ryania is effective in controlling the European corn borer and other worms. It is made from ground stems and roots of a South American shrub.

- Crushed tomato leaves work well for leaf spot diseases. They contain solanine, a chemical that has an inhibiting effect on black soft fungus. Simply grind two cups of leaves to a puree, add five pints of water and one ounce of cornstarch, and you have an effective spray-on solution. Keep it refrigerated.

- Tobacco water works great to kill fungus gnats, symphylids, centipedes, root lice, and other underground pests. Simply mix a solution of tobacco and water until it comes out the color of brown tea, then spray it on. Cigar and cigarette butts will also kill worms in the soil of household plants.

- Snuff works great for killing tiny flies and worms in the soil of household plants. Be sure not to use homemade tobacco remedies on tomatoes, peppers, eggplants, and other members of the Solanum family. It could spread a tobacco virus to these plants.

- Retenone works well in killing Mexican bean beetle, aphids, thrips, and chewing insects on contact. It is produced from derris, a plant found in Central and South America. Be careful though; it is toxic to fish and nesting birds.

- Hot peppers work well to keep dogs, cats, snails, and many insect pests away from your plants. Simply dust the powdered hot pepper on the plants or spray hot pepper sauce on them.

- Oil and sulfur sprays work well for killing insects on "hard" or woody plants. There are, however, two types to use, depending on the season:

    1.) Dormant oil is used when the plants are dormant, usually in winter or early spring.

    2.) Summer oil should be used only during the growing season and applied only to woody plants.

  Miscible oil sprays kill insects and eggs such as overwintering leaf rollers and aphid and mite eggs. It also works well on scale insects and adult mites. Follow the manufacturer's directions and dilute with water. (Source: *Mother Earth News,* February/March 1994.)

Water Smartly

Inefficiently watering your lawn wastes water, money, and energy. Here are some water conservation tips for your lawn:

- Water early or late in the day when the sun is not full, to avoid evaporation. About a third of the water sprinkled during the heat of the day is evaporated.
- Carefully position hoses and sprinklers to avoid watering unnecessary spots such as the sidewalk.
- Apply water slowly to prevent runoff.
- It is better to water thoroughly but infrequently to help your plants develop a deep root system for dry summer months.
- Mulch is a great way to inhibit weeds, prevent erosion, and retain moisture, and therefore conserve water. (Do not use peat moss. After drying, it prevents rainfall from reaching the soil.)
- Control weeds; why water unnecessary plants? (Source: *Consumer Reports,* May 1993.)

Water-Saving Hoses

If you need to water an odd-shaped area such as a narrow strip of grass or a winding flower bed, a soaker hose or sprinkler hose could be your best bet. Instead of using a normal sprinkler that will water everything around a specific area, thus wasting water, use the much more efficient soaker hose or a sprinkler hose. A soaker hose is a black, spongy-looking hose that oozes water and soaks the ground within a few inches of the hose. A sprinkler hose has tiny holes all over it that spray water about 6 to 12 feet from the hose. If the area you want to water isn't close to a faucet, both hoses hook to the end of a conventional hose as a sprinkler would. Each hose costs between $10 and $15 at your garden supply store.

Squeeze Nozzle

A squeeze nozzle is a great way to cut down on water use when watering the lawn and garden. The nozzle is made to restrict the amount of water that sprays out of your hose. It is also very convenient when washing a car or house; you don't have to turn off the faucet for washing or rinsing. A squeeze nozzle costs about $5 and should cut down your watering expenses by 20–40 percent.

Water Timers

Water timers are a great way to prevent water waste. They stop forgetful gardeners from letting the water run unnecessarily. Mechanical timers turn the water off after the time selected has lapsed, and electronic models let you program the day, starting time, and stopping time. Mechanical timers cost about $15, compared to electronic timers which run from $43 to $88.

Water-Conserving Plants

A great way to conserve water in your lawn or garden is to plant plants that do well in drought conditions. The following plants need very little water to survive; therefore, they conserve water you would be using on other plants:

- Native shrubs: bayberries, butterfly weed, Joe Pye weed, Coreopsis, calliopsis, and rudbeckias.

- Plants with gray foliage, many of which are native to dry climates, such as lavender, lamb's ear, mini artemisias and achilleas, and silver leafed salvia. These plants need lots of sun to survive, so if your lawn or garden is shaded they may not thrive.

- The common yucca, which is hardy in most of the United States, can withstand extreme summers and winters as well as months of drought.

- Plants with succulent leaves such as sedums and sempervivums.

- Plants with waxy leaves such as the Madagascar periwinkle.

- Clover is another great plant that will remain green long after weeks of drought turn turf grass brown.

Cleaning Up

For those of you who don't compost, try not to use non-biodegradable plastic trash bags that slow the decomposition of yard wastes. Instead, use large paper bags—they will biodegrade with your yard wastes.

10 Odds and Ends

This chapter, as its title suggests, contains all the products, tips, and other useful information that do not fit elsewhere in the book. It also informs the reader about many of our environmental issues, either through statistics or a discussion of the problem.

Too Much Waste

Every year, Americans throw away 18 billion disposable diapers, 2 billion razors and blades, 2 billion batteries, 220 million tires, 12 million tons of glass, 10 million tons of plastic ... altogether about 195 million tons of trash each year, or about 4.3 pounds per person each day.

"Throw it away," the proverbial expression used for trash, can no longer be tolerated because, after all, there is really no "away." Contrary to popular belief, discarded trash doesn't disappear. It is either buried in a landfill, incinerated, dumped in the ocean, or shipped away. So next time you go to discard trash in the dumpster, remember to articulate, "putting it somewhere else" or "relocating it" instead of "throwing it away." The problems have finally gotten to the point where the current out-of-sight, out-of-mind mentality is no longer appropriate.

The problems associated with our current methods of dealing with excessive waste could constitute a whole book, if not a volume of books, on the topic. In short, landfills are full and are polluting ground water, incinerator ash is releasing toxic chemicals into the air and water, and our refuse is harming marine life. America has simply run out of spaces to put our heaps of garbage.

Where Our Garbage Goes
In the United States, 80 percent of all garbage ends up in landfills, another 10 percent is burned, and only 10 percent is recycled.

Filling the Twin Towers
Americans throw away enough glass bottles and jars to fill both of New York's 1,350-foot World Trade Center's twin towers every two weeks.

(Source: Environmental Defense Fund.)

Not in My Backyard
States that *shipped away* the most toxins in 1992 (measured in millions of pounds):

Illinois: 165.5

Ohio: 141.8

Louisiana: 141.5

Texas: 116.9

Missouri: 107.9

States that *received* the most toxins in 1992 (measured in millions of pounds):

Pennsylvania: 195.0

Indiana: 186.0

Texas: 183.1

Illinois: 175.2

Ohio: 163.0

(Source: *USA Today* analysis of Environmental Protection Agency data.)

The Most Polluting States

The following ten states released the most toxic chemicals in 1992 (measured in millions of pounds):

Louisiana: 463.1

Texas: 417.1

Tennessee: 193.8

Ohio: 142.5

Indiana: 123.0

Mississippi: 118.7

Illinois: 117.0

Alabama: 111.8

North Carolina: 101.5

Kansas: 86.5

(Source: *USA Today* analysis of Environmental Protection Agency data.)

Recycling Creates More Jobs

Recycling your garbage creates six times as many jobs as landfilling.
(Source: *The Denver Post* 1991 Colorado Recycling Guide.)

End Junk Mail

Each year, the average American receives the equivalent of 1½ trees worth of junk mail. About 44 percent of it is never even opened! The simplest solution to this waste is to write to: Mail Preference Service, Direct Marketing Association, 6 East 43rd St., New York, NY 10017. Do this and your name will be removed from most mail order lists.

Deadly Newspapers

Each week, 500,000 trees (almost a whole forest) are cut down for Sunday newspapers. One solution to this problem is not to read anymore. But more realistically, recycle and buy recycled paper products whenever you can.

How Long Will it Take to Decompose?

It takes two to four weeks for a traffic ticket to decompose.
A cotton rag takes one to five months.
A plastic six-pack ring takes more than 450 years.
An aluminum can can take as much as 200 to 500 years.
(Source: Washington Citizens for Recycling.)

Two Cheers for Seattle, a Boo for NYC

Seattle has the highest recycling rate for any large American city. It currently recycles 34 percent of its solid waste and 77 percent of its residential waste. New York City, on the other hand, recycles only 6 to 8 percent of its trash and its residents throw away an average of 6 pounds per person daily.

Our Landfills are Stuffed

Americans are running out of space to put our garbage. Currently, fewer than 4,000 of the 14,000 landfills that were in operation in 1977 are still in operation. By the year 2000, that number is expected to drop to a mere 1,800. At the rate we generate garbage, 500 new landfills are needed each year.

America's High Energy Use

The average American uses the same amount of energy as do 3 Japanese, 6 Mexicans, 13 Chinese, 35 Indians, 153 Bangladeshis, or 499 Ethiopians.
(Source: Zero Population Growth, Washington, DC.)

Fossil Fuel Use
Fossil fuels are being depleted 100,000 times faster than they are being formed.
(Source: Energy for Planet Earth, Readings from *Scientific American,* 1990.)

Renewable Energy
According to the Union of Concerned Scientists, 80 percent of government funding for the research and development of renewable energy technologies has been cut in the last decade.

Not Using Renewable Energy Enough
Of the total amount of energy used in the United States, only 7.5 percent is from renewable energy sources.
(Source: Union of Concerned Scientists.)

No Electricity at All

Approximately 1.7 billion people, or 33 percent of the world's population, have no electricity at all.
(Source: Union of Concerned Scientists.)

Deaths Due to Air Pollution

An estimated 50,000 people die prematurely in the United States and Canada each year as a result of cardiac or respiratory problems attributed to air pollution levels.
(Source: Greenpeace Action.)

Books or Trash

For many American schools, trash disposal is as expensive as the money spent on textbooks.
(Source: *The Denver Post,* 1991 Colorado Recycling Guide.)

Clearing Our Land for Livestock

In the United States, 220 million acres of land have been deforested for livestock production. About 25 million acres (about the size of Austria) have been deforested in Brazil, and half the forests in Central America have been cleared solely for beef production. Believe it or not, a third of North America is devoted to livestock production.
(Source: *50 Simple Things You Can Do To Save The Earth,* Earth Works Press, 1989.)

Grazed to Death

Over 5 million cattle have died in sub-Saharan Africa as a result of overgrazing and desertification of land.
(Source: *Global Environmental Issues,* Routledge Publishers.)

What Lives in the Rain Forest?

- 45 percent of all the world's flowering plants (112,000 species)
- 30 percent of all birds (2,700 species)
- 90 percent of all primates (203 species)
- Around 30 million distinct species of insects
  (Source: Conservation International.)

Unprotected Tropical Forests
Less than 5 percent of the world's tropical forests are protected in parks or reserves.
(Source: "The Death of Birth," Linden, E., *Time,* Jan. 2, 1989. New York, NY, pp. 32–35.)

The Loss of Animals

Our Largest Animal Is Threatened
Whales are perhaps the most amazing creatures of the sea due to their sheer size. Unfortunately, due to commercial whaling and overhunting they are threatened with extinction. More whales were killed during the first 40 years of the twentieth century than the total killed during the preceding four centuries. In 1962, the number of whales killed worldwide peaked at over 62,000. Due to the shrinking numbers of whales the catch shrank drastically during the 1960s and 1970s. By 1980, only about 15,000 whales were killed. According to Greenpeace Action, just in Australia's Southern Ocean, the original whale population of around 250,000 has shrunk to a mere 200.

Chimpanzees
Since chimpanzees are strikingly similar to humans, their huge demand as research animals and for other purposes has

created a serious threat to the animal's survival. Humans also hunt chimpanzees for export to research institutions, circuses, and zoos, and for food or for use as household pets. Chimpanzees are also threatened by humans due to development of the grassy plains and forests they once inhabited. Conservation is prevalent in some African countries where game preserves have been established to protect the endangered chimpanzees.
(Source: World Book Encyclopedia.)

Poaching Our Largest Land Animal

Once roaming throughout Africa, the African elephant is now found only south of the Sahara. Due to poaching for ivory and the destruction of the elephant's habitat for human development, the existence of our largest land animal is threatened. Since the 1970s the elephant population in Tanzania has dropped from nearly 250,000 to a mere 61,000; Uganda's from around 20,000 to barely 1,600; and Kenya's from 140,000 to maybe 16,000 in 1989.

The average adult African bull elephant weighs 6.3 tons and stands 10 feet 6 inches at the shoulders. According to the Guinness Book of World Records the largest one ever measured was around 13 feet and weighed an astonishing 13.5 tons.

Wolves

Once roaming throughout North America, wolves are an endangered species in every state except Minnesota (where they are threatened) and Alaska. During the mid-1980s an estimated 6,000 to 10,000 wolves lived in Alaska and only about 1,300 elsewhere in the United States, mostly in Minnesota. Their populations have greatly declined due to loss of habitat from human development and the hatred many people have for them. Many ranchers hunt and trap wolves because they threaten their livestock, and disgruntled hunters kill wolves because they feed on game animals. There are, however, many groups that are trying to reintroduce wolves into their state.

Organizations for Wolves

Mission Wolf, P.O. Box 211, Silver Cliff, CO 81249, (719) 746-2919

North American Wolf Society, P.O. Box 82950, Fairbanks, AK 99708, (907) 474-6117

Sinapu, P.O. Box 3243, Boulder, CO 80307, (303) 494-7920

Five Billion and Counting

There are about 5.6 billion members of the human family on the earth. Every year, another 145 million or so more people are born. This averages about 12 million per month, 2.7 million per week, 395,000 per day, 16,000 per hour, 275 per minute, and 4.6 per second.

About 51 million people die each year, or about 1.6 per second, leaving a natural increase of about 93 million people a year, or about 3 per second.

(Source: Population Reference Bureau's 1990 World Population Data Sheet, *The World Almanac and Book of Facts*, 1995.)

Population Doubling Rate

Europe has a population of 495 million and a doubling time of 272 years.

North America's population of 270 million has a doubling time of 101 years.

The Commonwealth of Independent States (the former

Soviet Union) has a population of 284 million and a doubling time of 79 years.

Australia, New Zealand, and the South Pacific islands have a population of 25 million and a doubling time of 59 years.

Asia's population of 2.9 billion has a doubling time of 37 years.

Latin America's population of 421 million has a doubling time of 31 years.

Africa's population of 601 million has a doubling time of 24 years.

(Source: Population Reference Bureau, Inc., 1987.)

A Million More People

Every four days the world's population increases by a million people.

Our Crowded Planet in 2060

Those newborns who arrived in 1990 will live on a crowded planet when they reach age 70. The world's population in 1990 was 5.3 billion and will increase to 10.8 billion by 2060.

(Source: Population Reference Bureau.)

Oil Spills

Worst Assault on the Environment

On January 19, 1989, Iraqi president Saddam Hussein ordered the pumping of Gulf crude oil from Kuwait's Sea Island terminal and from seven massive tankers into the Persian Gulf. An estimated four to six million barrels (126 to 189 million gallons) poured into the Persian Gulf, where they caught fire. After nine months of exhausting work, the fires were finally extinguished.

Biggest Oil Spill

The biggest oil spill that ever occurred resulted from a marine blowout beneath the drilling of *Ixtoc I* in the Gulf of Campeche, Gulf of Mexico, on June 3, 1979. It was finally capped March 24, 1980, after 94.5 million gallons of oil leaked into the gulf.

Exxon *Valdez*

On March 24, 1989, the Exxon *Valdez* struck a reef in Prince William Sound, Alaska, spilling 10 million gallons of crude oil. Oil spread over a total of 2,600 square miles. Believe it or not, Americans dump 10 to 20 times more motor oil per year than was spilled by the Exxon *Valdez*!

Pollution Causes Shutdown of World's Largest City

On March 17, 1992, air pollution shut down Mexico City for the first time in history. The world's largest city, home to more than 16 million people, had to close down schools for the day, order industries to reduce operations (225 industries cut production by 50–70 percent), and ban almost half of all cars from the streets.

Nuclear Testing Deaths

In 1992, about 430,000 people died from cancers resulting from radiation exposure from nuclear testing. (Source: Greenpeace.)

Disposing of Hazardous Materials

Now that you know what materials in your house are toxic, the question arises, "What do I do with them?"

The following is a list of hazardous products and recommendations on how to get rid of them safely.

• Aerosol Cans—Keep away from heat, high pressure, and flames. Also, make sure all aerosol cans are empty before throwing them away, so they don't explode when crushed in the garbage truck or compactor.

• Ammonia and Ammonia-based cleaners—The best way to get rid of these wastes is to dilute them with lots of water and flush slowly down the drain. Do not put them in the trash or mix with bleach; deadly gases may result.

• Antifreeze, Automotive Fluids—Take these products to a hazardous waste collection site, recycling center, or service station. Do not pour down drains, on the ground, or in the trash; they will greatly pollute ground water.

• Auto Waxes and Polishes, Body Filler, and Road Salts— If you can't use up the product, give it to someone who can or take it to a collection program.

• Barbecue Lighter Fluid—Do not store the unused portion in your home; the fumes are toxic. Either give unused portions to a friend to use or take them to a collection site. Do not incinerate cans or throw in garbage.

• Batteries—Batteries contain many hazardous substances. Nickel, cadmium, mercury, and alkali are harmful to people, animals, and fish. Be sure to recycle auto batteries at a battery retailer, hearing-aid batteries at a hospital, and mercury batteries at a hazardous-waste center. They will explode if put in a stove or open fire.

- Chlorine Bleach—To dispose of chlorine bleach, dilute with lots of water and pour slowly down the drain or toilet. Never mix with ammonia!
- Disinfectants and Drain Cleaners—Only very small amounts can be put down the drain, and only if diluted with large amounts of water.

Making a Difference With Your Idea

If millions of Americans came up with one or two little environment-friendly ideas, just imagine the impact it would have. Certainly every one of us has many such thoughts throughout the course of a year. We think of a small but significant idea, but because we don't have the resources to implement it, we forget it. Well, from now on, here's a way you can do something about it.

Recently an idea came to me while brushing my teeth. Looking at my toothbrush, I thought: "What a waste of plastic it is to throw away an entire toothbrush when its brush wears down. It would be much more economical if the worn out brush were replaced with a new one." Of course, I don't own a business that can manufacture, market, and distribute such a product, so I was not about to start a company to manufacture toothbrush refills. What I did, however, was pass my idea on to a toothbrush manufacturer. But before submitting my idea, under the advice of a patent attorney, I forwarded the following confidential disclosure agreement letter to several different manufacturers.

Confidential Disclosure Agreement Letter

I am in the possession of certain confidential ideas and information relating to_____(insert a short title describing the subject matter of the information), which I refer to as my trade secrets. It is my wish, as well as yours, that I disclose these trade secrets to you so that you may evaluate them to determine whether you wish to discuss a business relationship for our mutual benefit. It is my desire to convey the trade secrets to you if you will treat it as valuable proprietary trade secret information and maintain it in confidence.

Thus, I am willing to disclose the information and I understand you wish to have the opportunity to evaluate it on the following basis.

You agree not to disclose this confidential, proprietary, trade secret information to anyone other than those who reasonably need to know of it for purposes of making your evaluation. Furthermore, you agree that you will at no time disclose these trade secrets to anyone outside of your organization and will not use this information for commercial purposes, except for your evaluation, unless you have my express written consent, or unless the trade secrets have already, or at any time in the future, become part of the public domain or been publicly disclosed by someone having a right to make such a public disclosure, or information has been or is in the future disclosed to you by a third party who is lawfully in possession of the trade secrets and has a right to disclose them to you.

Date of Signature	Your Name

Date of Signature	Name of Company Officer	Title

My cover letter indicated I had an environment-friendly idea that was economically sound for the company and the consumer. I stated that my idea would give the company an advantage over its competition. Who knows, the right company could respond to such an idea and it might pay off for you. It's certainly worth a try—and you have nothing to lose.

Whether or not an idea of this nature ever makes money for me or you is another matter. It does, however, open a window that could make a difference. As my father always told me, "Ideas are a dime a dozen but the men and women who implement them are priceless."

11 Getting Involved

hink globally, act locally" isn't just an expression that stops in your home. This chapter is about how you can really get involved. Too many people just sit there and complain about our environmental problems without getting out there to ease them. Either by writing your elected officials or joining an environmental organization, you can make a difference. Unlike most of the preceding chapters in this book, this one goes beyond making a difference on an individual basis; the first section will teach you how to write an influential letter to your congressman, and the second part gives information on the major environmental organizations so you can join others who want to make a difference on the same issues and causes.

Writing Your Congressman

When was the last time you wrote to your congressman? Too many people complain about Congress, but when it comes down to it, more than 90 percent of Americans go their entire lives without expressing an opinion to the person who represents them in Congress. In order for your congressmen to keep in touch with how the people in their district feel, they must get mail telling them. And congressmen do listen. After all, their constituents are voters. For every letter they receive, they know there are several hundred other people who feel the same way but are too lazy to write.

Getting Through the Door

The chances of getting your mail read by a congressman will substantially increase if you comply with the following suggestions.

1. Be sure to address it properly: "Hon. _____, House Office Building, Washington, D.C. 20515" or "Senator _____, Senate Office Building, Washington, D.C., 20510."

2. Identify the bill or issue. About 20,000 bills are introduced each year in Congress; try to be specific by stating its bill number or its popular title.

3. Send it on time. Make sure your letter arrives before the bill is out of the committee, or has passed the House. Inform your congressman while there is adequate time to take action.

4. Send your letters to the representative of your district or the senators of your state. There is a "congressional courtesy" procedure that all letters be forwarded to the congressman in the proper district. So writing to another person in another district will usually mean just taking a little longer to get to the congressman in your district.

5. Keep your letter brief and to the point. There is simply not time enough to completely read all letters. You will have a better chance of being heard if you keep the letter short and concise. Handwritten letters are alright if they are legible. The form, phraseology, and grammar are completely unimportant.

Influencing Your Congressman

Writing a letter to your congressman is just the first step in making a difference. *Influencing* your congressman is what really counts. Your letters may not be read by the congressmen themselves, but their staff will inform them how the mail is running. This may be beneficial on environmental matters because many staff members are younger and more in touch with the environment than the rest of Congress. The following suggestions will sharpen the impact of your letter.

1. Write your own views—not someone else's. A personal letter will have a much greater impact than a form letter or a signature on a petition. Your congressman already knows the position of the major lobbying groups and that many people sign a petition, without ever really reading it, just to avoid offending the circulator. He or she doesn't, however, know your views until you write.

2. Give your reasons for taking a stand. Your letter will have much more of an impact if you state personal reasons for taking a stand instead of just stating that you oppose it. Mention how the bill will personally affect your business or home.

3. Be constructive. Tell your congressman an alternative way to approach something instead of just opposing it.

4. If you have expert knowledge on an issue, share it with your congressman. He or she can simply not be an expert on everything and will take your advice much more seriously if you know what you are talking about.

5. Ask your congressman to give you a position on the matter. If he or she is noncommittal on the issue, write back and request a responsive answer. The environment is going to suffer until the constituents get commitments from congressmen on specific legislative principles.

Environmental Organizations

Acting as a group can increase the pressure on those who would endanger our environment more than you may think. The following organizations have done an extraordinary job working for the causes they believe in. Hence, supporting them will support the cause you believe in.

Acid Rain Foundation
1410 Varsity Dr.
Raleigh, NC 27606
(919) 828-9443
The Acid Rain Foundation's purpose is to foster a greater understanding of global atmospheric issues by raising the level of public awareness, supplying educational resources, and supporting research. The membership fee is $35 per year and includes the quarterly publication, *The Acid Rain Update.* Its annual revenue is $100,000 and is spent on: administration, 24 percent; fundraising, 9 percent; programs, 67 percent.

Adopt a Stream Foundation
P.O. Box 5558
Everett, WA 98206
(206) 388-3313

Adopt a Stream Foundation promotes environmental awareness and stream enhancement. The foundation provides all the support and guidance necessary for those who wish to adopt a stream. Membership is $10 and up for volunteer-run organizations and includes a membership to the quarterly newsletter, *Streamlines*.

African Wildlife Foundation
1717 Massachusetts Ave. NW
Washington, DC 20036
(202) 265-8393; fax (202) 265-2361

The African Wildlife Foundation's purpose is to save endangered African wildlife and other natural resources. Founded in 1961, the foundation now has over 100,000 members. A tax-deductible annual fee of $15 includes a subscription to their 12-page annual news journal, *Wildlife News,* describing conservation issues in Africa, unique gift items available only through *Wildlife News,* opportunities to go on an African safari, and a bumper sticker saying "Only Elephants Should Wear Ivory."

American Forest Association
P.O. Box 2000
Washington, DC 20013
(202) 667-3300

The American Forest Association works to promote awareness in forest conservation and tree planting and for the maintenance and improvement of the health of our trees and forests. Annual membership is $24 and includes a subscription to *American Forests,* a bimonthly magazine.

American Rivers
801 Pennsylvania Ave. SE, Suite 400
Washington, DC 20003
(202) 547-6900

American Rivers is dedicated to preserving our nation's rivers and landscapes. Annual membership is $20 and up and includes their quarterly newsletter, *American Rivers,* along with a long list of outfitters who support river conservation.

American Wildlands
40 East Main St., Suite 2
Bozeman, MT 59715
(406) 586-8175

American Wildlands is a conservation organization dedicated to promoting ecologically sustainable uses of public wildlife resources, including forests, wilderness, wildlife, fisheries, and rivers. Annual membership is $25 and up and includes *On the Wild Side,* a quarterly newsletter.

Center for Marine Conservation
1725 DeSales St. NW, Suite 500
Washington, DC 20036
(202) 429-5609

The Center for Marine Conservation, formerly the Center of Environmental Education, aims to protect marine wildlife and their habitats and to conserve coastal and ocean resources. Annual membership is $20 and includes the quarterly newsletter *Marine Conservation News,* legislative updates, and "Action Alerts" outlining ways people can support marine conservation.

Co-op America
2100 M St. NW, Suite 403
Washington, DC 20063
(202) 872-5307; toll free(800) 424-2667

Co-op America provides alternatives to educate customers on environmentally safe products, on investing in environmentally friendly businesses, on which corporate polluters to boycott, and how to demand change. They encourage people to let their money do the voting to help create an environmentally sound economy. A $20 annual fee makes you a member and entitles you to receive a copy of *Shopping For a Better World*, copies of Co-op America's *Alternative Catalog*, a subscription to *The Co-op America Quarterly*, a copy of their *Socially Responsible Financial Planning Guide*, a copy of *Co-op America's Directory*, optional use of their investment services, optional health and insurance plans, optional use of their Travel Links travel agency, and an optional Visa card, offered through a bank that has a fund devoted to social and environmental investments.

The Cousteau Society
930 West 21st St.
Norfolk, VA 23517
Regional offices in Los Angeles, CA; New York, NY; Paris, France
(804) 627-1144; fax (804) 627-7547

The Cousteau Society was founded by the famous environmentalist and underwater explorer Captain Jacques-Yves Cousteau in 1973 to help protect and improve the quality of life for present and future generations. The organization has around 330,000 members. A $20 tax-deductible annual membership includes a monthly subscription to the *Calypso Log* (children receive *Dolphin Log*) and many other opportunities available only to members of The Cousteau Society.

Defenders of Wildlife
1244 19th St. NW
Washington, DC 20036
(202) 659-9510; fax (202) 833-3349

Defenders of Wildlife is a nonprofit organization dedicated to protecting wildlife in their habitat. Defenders utilizes public education, litigation, and advocacy of progressive public policies to defend the diversity of wildlife. Membership is $20 and includes the bimonthly magazine *Defenders,* voting privileges for the Board of Directors, and eligibility for the organization's Visa or MasterCard. It also publishes annual endangered species reports, educational newsletters, and citizen action alerts. Its annual revenue is $4,345,902 and is spent on: administration, 13 percent; programs, 64 percent; membership, 10 percent; other, 13 percent.

Ducks Unlimited, Inc.
1 Waterfowl Way
Long Grove, IL 60047
(312) 438-4300

Ducks Unlimited raises money for developing, preserving, restoring, and maintaining the waterfowl habitat in North America. Membership is $20 and includes a subscription to the monthly magazine *Ducks Unlimited.* Its annual revenue is $63,000,000 and is used on: administration, 3.8 percent; fundraising, 17.9 percent; programs, 76.3 percent; other, 2 percent.

EarthSave
P.O. Box 949
Felton, CA 95018
(408) 423-4069

EarthSave is dedicated to an ecologically sustainable future through educating people to adopt a more healthful and environmentally sound diet, buy nonpolluting energy supplies, and adopt wiser use of natural resources. The organization was developed from the work of John Robbins, author of *Diet for a New America* and *May All be Fed: Diet for a New World.* Membership is $20 to $35 a year and includes the Project EarthSave newsletter and periodic notices and updates of current activities.

Earthwatch
P.O. Box 403N, 680 Mt. Auburn St.
Watertown, MA 02172
(617) 926-8200; toll free (800) 776-0188; fax (617) 926-8532
Earthwatch sends volunteers to work with scientists around the world who are working to save rainforests and endangered species, preserve archaeological finds, and study pollution effects. Its membership fees are $25 a year, including six issues a year of *Earthwatch* magazine. Its annual revenue is spent on: administration, 16 percent; fundraising, 4 percent; programs, 80 percent.

Environmental Action, Inc.
1525 New Hampshire Ave. NW
Washington, DC 20036
(202) 745-4870
Environmental Action, Inc., lobbies Congress for passage of strong environmental laws such as the Clean Air Act Superfund. The organization works closely with citizen groups on topics such as recycling, right-to-know laws, and toxic pollution. Membership is $20 per year and includes *Environmental Action Magazine,* a bimonthly publication that provides in-depth articles on subjects such as solid waste, plastic containers, and ecotourism.

Environmental Defense Fund
257 Park Avenue South
New York, NY 10010
(212) 505-2375; fax (212) 505-2375

The Environmental Defense Fund was founded in 1967 by a group of scientists, economists, and lawyers to defend the environment. The organization focuses on water pollution, pesticides, wildlife preservation, wetland protection, rain forests, the ozone layer, acid rain, and toxic chemicals and waste. Membership is $20 per year and includes a quarterly subscription to *EDF Newsletter.* Its annual revenues of $18,500,000 are used on: administration, 3 percent; fundraising, 13 percent; programs, 82 percent; other, 2 percent.

Friends of Animals
P.O. Box 1244
Norwalk, CT 06856
(203) 866-5223

Friends of Animals' purpose is to eliminate human brutality to animals. The organization has programs in areas such as breeding control, eliminating animal experimentation and testing, humane use of farm animals, and a wild animal orphanage and rehabilitation center in Liberia. The organization also heads the Committee for Humane Legislation, which plays a key role in legislative affairs. Membership is $20 per year.

Friends of the Earth
218 D St. SE
Washington, DC 20003
(202) 544-2600; fax (202) 543-4710

Friends of the Earth promotes the conservation, protection, and rational use of the earth. Its activities include lobbying in Washington, DC, and many other state capitals and networking public information on environmental issues. Membership is $25 for individuals and a student/low income/senior rate of $15. Membership includes the monthly magazine *Not Man Apart.*

Greenpeace
1436 U St. NW
Washington, DC 20009
(202) 462-1177; fax (202) 462-4507

Greenpeace is an international environmental organization dedicated to protecting the environment and all its life supports. Greenpeace has focused its efforts on halting the needless killing of marine animals and other endangered species, ocean ecology, toxic waste reduction, and nuclear disarmament. Greenpeace was founded in 1971 and has four million members. Membership is $20 and includes the bimonthly *Greenpeace* magazine.

Greenpeace's annual revenue of $50,000,000 is used on: administration, 3 percent; fundraising, 19 percent; programs, 78 percent.

Humane Society of the United States
2100 L St. NW
Washington, DC 20037
(202) 452-1100

The Humane Society of the United States provides resources to the general public on topics such as animal control, cruelty investigation, publications, and human education. Membership is $10 a year.

Institute for Earth Education
Box 288
Warrenville, IL 60555
(312) 393-3096

The Institute for Earth Education is focused entirely on educating people on the environmental crisis of the earth. The institute is committed to supporting and developing earth education programs. Membership is $20 per year and includes a quarterly journal, *Talking Leaves*. The institute's *Sourcebook*, outlining the group's Earth Education program, and program materials are free upon request.

International Council for Bird Preservation
801 Pennsylvania Ave. SE
Washington DC 20003
(202) 778-9563

The International Council for Bird Preservation was formed to help maintain the diversity, distribution, abundance, and natural habitats of bird species worldwide. They also work to prevent the extinction of any bird species or subspecies. Membership is $35 and up and includes two quarterly magazines, *World Bird Watch* and *U.S. Bird News*.

Izaak Walton League of America
1401 Wilson Blvd., Level B
Arlington, VA 22209
(703) 528-1818; fax (703) 528-1836

The Izaak Walton League of America was established to protect America's soil, air, woods, waters, and wildlife. It is currently emphasizing clean air, clean water, energy efficiency, wildlife habitat protection, improved public land management, and outdoor ethics. Membership dues are $20 a year and include a quarterly magazine, *Outdoor America*. It has an annual revenue of $2,000,000 which is used on: administration, 11 percent; fundraising, 13 percent; programs, 76 percent.

League of Conservation Voters
320 4th St. NE
Washington, DC 20002
(202) 785-8683

The League of Conservation Voters is a nonpartisan political group for the environmental movement. Its purpose is to elect pro-environmental candidates to Congress, based on energy, environment, and natural resources issues. Annual membership is $25 and includes *The National Environmental Scorecard,* an annual rating of members of Congress on environmental issues.

League of Women Voters
1730 M St. NW
Washington, DC 20036
(202) 429-1965

The League of Women Voters is a nonpartisan, political organization dedicated to influencing public policy through education and advocacy, and encouraging citizen action in government. The league focuses on social issues and environmental issues such as air and water quality, solid- and hazardous-waste management, land use and energy. An annual national membership is $50 (local memberships vary). It includes a subscription to the *National Voter* magazine, a monthly publication.

National Arbor Day Foundation
100 Arbor Ave.
Nebraska City, NE 68410
(402) 474-5655

The National Arbor Day Foundation's main purpose is to encourage tree planting and conservation. The foundation provides information and materials for cities to plan their own Arbor Day celebrations. Annual membership is $10 and includes a subscription to their monthly newsletter, *Arbor Day,* and a tree book.

National Audubon Society
950 Third Ave.
New York, NY 10022
(212) 832-3200

The National Audubon Society was founded in 1905 and now has around 550,000 members. The society works to protect wildlife and wildlife habitat through research, education, and political action. Membership to the society is $30 per year and includes various bonuses such as a subscription to *Audubon* magazine, free visits to Audubon Nature Centers, and opportunities to buy nature-oriented books, gifts, and artwork.

National Coalition Against the Misuse of Pesticides
530 7th St. SE
Washington, DC 20003
(202) 543-5450

The National Coalition Against the Misuse of Pesticides is dedicated to educating individuals, organizations, and communities about pesticides and their alternatives. Membership is $20 per year and includes their newsletter, *Pesticides and You.*

National Geographic Society
17th and M Sts. NW
Washington, DC 20036
(202) 857-7000

The National Geographic Society was founded in 1888 and now has over 10.8 million members. The society is a nonprofit organization dedicated to global ecology and environmental research. Annual membership is $21 and includes a subscription to *National Geographic* magazine.

National Parks and Conservation Association
1015 31st St. NW, Suite 400
Washington, DC 20007
(202) 944-8530

The National Parks and Conservation Association works to protect, promote, and improve our National Park System while educating the public about the parks. A tax-deductible annual membership of $25 includes a subscription to *National Parks* magazine and many other benefits.

National Recycling Coalition
1101 30th St. NW, Suite 305
Washington, DC 20007
(202) 625-6406

The National Recycling Coalition is dedicated to maximizing recycling and conservation as integral components of waste and resource management, through education, information, and lobbying. Annual membership is $30 and includes their bimonthly newsletter, *NRC Connection.*

National Toxics Campaign
37 Temple Pl., 4th Fl.
Boston, MA 02111
(617) 482-1477

The National Toxics Campaign works to bring citizens together to implement preventive solutions to the nation's toxic waste problem. They concentrate on Superfund activities. Membership is $25 a year for an individual and $50 and up for community groups. Membership includes their quarterly magazine, *Toxic Times,* and access to their testing lab to determine toxicity of soil, water, and food in communities.

National Wildlife Federation
1400 16th St. NW
Washington, DC 20036
(202) 797-6800; fax (202) 797-6646

The National Wildlife Federation is an environmental education association promoting the responsible use of natural resources and protection of the global environment. It distributes educational materials and periodicals, sponsors education programs in conservation, and litigates environmental disputes in an effort to conserve fisheries, wildlife, and natural resources. Membership dues vary depending on magazine subscription. It is $15 per year for *National Wildlife* and *International Wildlife* monthly subscriptions; $14 for *Ranger Rick,* a monthly magazine for children 6 to 12 years old; and $10 for a monthly subscription to *Your Backyard,* an environmental magazine for children 3 to 5 years old. The National Wildlife Federation's annual revenue is $92,000,000, and is used on: programs, 68 percent; membership, 21 percent; administration/fundraising, 11 percent.

Natural Resources Defense Council
40 West 20th St.
New York, NY 10011
(212) 727-2700

The Natural Resources Defense Council is dedicated to issues such as air and water pollution, climate, toxic substances, and energy and natural resource conservation. Annual membership dues are $10 and include a subscription to *The Amicus Journal* (quarterly) and their bimonthly newsletter, the *Natural Resources Defense Council Newsline.*

The Nature Conservancy
1815 North Lynn St.
Arlington, VA 22209
(703) 841-5300

The Nature Conservancy acts to preserve ecosystems and the rare species and communities they shelter. It manages a system of more than 1,300 nature sanctuaries in all 50 states and maintains a database, the Heritage Network, which is a national inventory of species in each state. Membership is $15 and includes a bimonthly magazine, *The Nature Conservancy Magazine*, as well as newsletters and update information from state chapters. Its annual revenue of $16,000,000 is spent on: administration, 6.6 percent; fundraising, 3.9 percent; programs, 85 percent; membership, 4.5 percent.

Pacific Whale Foundation
101 North Kihei Rd., Suite 21
Kihei, Maui, HI 96753
(808) 879-8811; toll free (800) 942-5311
The Pacific Whale Foundation works on issues such as whale protection and preservation, ocean ecology, and water pollution. Annual membership is $15 for students and seniors, $20 for individuals, and $25 for families.

People for the Ethical Treatment of Animals
P.O. Box 42516
Washington, DC 20015-0516
(301) 770-7444
People for the Ethical Treatment of Animals is dedicated to ending the harsh treatment of animals, with a special focus on animals used in experimentation. Annual membership of $15 includes their bimonthly news magazine, *PETA News*. You also get a fact sheet on "Companies That Don't Conduct Animal Testing" and "Companies That Test On Animals."

Rachel Carson Council
8940 Jones Mill Rd.
Chevy Chase, MD 20815
(301) 652-1877

The Rachel Carson Council provides information on chemical use and ecology of the environment. Annual membership is $15 and includes a subscription to its newsletter and other Council publications.

Rainforest Alliance
270 Lafayette St., Suite 512
New York, NY 10012
(212) 941-1900

The Rainforest Alliance aims to link professional organizations, financial institutions, scientists, the business community, conservationists, and concerned citizens to support rainforest education, research, and acquisition. Membership is $15 per year for students and senior citizens, and $20 for individuals, and includes a subscription to *The Canopy, Hot Topics from the Tropics,* discounts on rainforest merchandise, and voting rights for electing members of the Board of Directors.

Renew America
1001 Connecticut Ave. NW, Suite 719
Washington, DC 20036
(202) 232-2252

Renew America is an educational network working towards efficient use of natural resources at federal, state, and private levels. Annual membership is $25 and includes the quarterly *Renew America Report* and a copy of the yearly *State of the States* report, which provides an annual "report card" on current developments across the nation.

Save The Redwoods League
114 Sansome St., Room 605
San Francisco, CA 94104
(415) 362-2352

Save The Redwoods League was established to rescue areas of old-growth forest from destruction. The league takes membership money to buy redwood groves for preservation. Annual membership starts at $10 and includes a spring and fall bulletin of the league's activities.

Sierra Club
730 Polk St.
San Francisco, CA 94109
(415) 776-2211

The Sierra Club was founded in 1892 by legendary environmentalist John Muir. It is dedicated to conserving the natural environment by influencing public policy decisions. Annual membership is $33 and includes a monthly subscription to *Sierra* magazine and other chapter publications.

Soil and Water Conservation Society of America
7515 NE Ankeny Rd.
Ankeny, IA 50021
(515) 289-2331

The Soil and Water Conservation Society of America is committed to the conservation of water, land, and other natural resources. The organization also sponsors a scholarship program for high school and college students. Membership is $25 for the first year and $37 thereafter. It includes the bimonthly *Journal of Soil and Water Conservation,* and a newsletter covering the annual meeting.

Student Conservation Association
P.O. Box 550
Charlestown, NH 03603
(603) 826-4301

The Student Conservation Association offers high school and college students the opportunity to volunteer their services for the better management of forests, public land, national parks, and natural resources. Annual membership is $10 for students, and $25 for others. It includes the annual programs listings and the newsletter *The Volunteer.*

TreePeople
12601 Mulholland Dr.
Beverly Hills, CA 90210
(818) 753-4600

TreePeople works to encourage personal involvement, community action, and global awareness on environmental issues. Membership is $25 and up a year and includes the bimonthly newsletter *Seedling News,* six free seedlings a year, and discounts on TreePeople T-shirts.

Trees for Life
1103 Jefferson
Wichita, KS 67203
(316) 263-7294

Trees for Life provides funding, management, and information on growing food-bearing trees for people in developing countries. Membership is free and includes their quarterly newsletter, *Life Times.*

U.S. Public Interest Research Group
215 Pennsylvania Ave. SE
Washington, DC 20003
(202) 546-9707

U.S. Public Interest Research Group focuses on consumer and environmental protection, energy policy, and governmental and corporate reform. Membership is $25 and includes the quarterly *Citizens Agenda.*

The Whale Center
3929 Piedmont Ave.

Oakland, CA 94611

(415) 654-6621

The Whale Center is dedicated to protecting whales and their habitats through education, research, conservation, and advocacy. Annual membership is $25 for individuals, $10 for students and seniors, $35 for families, and $250 for a lifetime membership. Membership includes the organization's quarterly newsletter, *The Whale Center Journal.*

The Wilderness Society
1400 Eye St. NW

Washington, DC 20005

(202) 842-3400

The Wilderness Society works to protect wildlands, wildlife, forests, parks, rivers, and shorelands. Annual membership is $15 for the first year and $30 thereafter and includes a subscription to *The Wildlifer,* a bimonthly newsletter.

Wildlife Conservation International
New York Zoological Society

Bronx, NY 10460

(212) 367-1010

Wildlife Conservation International is an international conservation program dedicated to wildlife protection and preservation. Annual membership dues are $23 for associates, $50 for supporting members, and include a subscription to the *Wildlife Conservation International Newsletter.*

World Resources Institute
1735 New York Ave. NW

Washington, DC 20006

(202) 638-6300

World Resources Institute helps the government, public, and organizations deal with issues in ecology, environmental degradation, and natural resource management. Each year the institute publishes the *World Resources Report.*

Worldwatch Institute
1776 Massachusetts Ave. NW
Washington, DC 20036
(202) 452-1999

Worldwatch Institute is an independent research organization alerting decision-makers and the general public to emerging global trends in the availability and management of both human and natural resources. It publishes the *State of the World* series. Worldwatch papers and books are available by subscription for $25 a year. It also publishes a bimonthly magazine, *World Watch,* for $20 a year.

World Wildlife Fund
1250 24th St. NW
Washington, DC 20037
(202) 293-4800

The World Wildlife Fund (WWF) was founded in 1961 and now is the world's largest international conservation organization with around 670,000 members. The organization works to protect the world's wildlife and the biological diversity they need to survive, placing special priority on the tropical rainforests in Asia, Latin America, and Africa. Annual membership of $15 includes *Focus,* their bimonthly newsletter, and letters regarding upcoming projects and travel programs.

Index